Havana-Miami

Havana-Miami

The U.S.-Cuba migration conflict

by Dr. Jesús Arboleya

Translated by Mary Todd

OCEAN PRESS

Cover design by David Spratt

ISBN 1-875284-91-5

First printed 1996

Printed in Australia

Published by Ocean Press,
GPO Box 3279, Melbourne, Victoria 3001, Australia
Fax: (61-3) 9372 1765

Distributed in the United States by the Talman Company,
    131 Spring Street, New York, NY 10012, USA
Distributed in Canada by Marginal Distribution,
    277 George St. N., Unit 102, Peterborough, Ontario K9J 3G9, Canada
Distributed in Britain and Europe by Central Books,
    99 Wallis Road, London E9 5LN, Britain
Distributed in Australia by Astam Books,
    57-61 John Street, Leichhardt, NSW 2040, Australia
Distributed in Cuba and Latin America by Ocean Press,
    Apartado 686, C.P. 11300, Havana, Cuba
Distributed in Southern Africa by Phambili Agencies,
    52 Jeppe Street, Johannesburg 2001, South Africa

Contents

✪

✪

Acknowledgments

My thanks to Fabián Escalante Font, Jacinto Almazán del Olmo and Mirta Muñiz, who read over the manuscript and made valuable suggestions; to Mary Todd, for her careful translation; to Conrado Peraza and Juan de Jesús Hidalgo-Gato, who helped edit the work; and to the rest of the comrades at the Center for National Security Studies, for their ongoing cooperation.

Dr. Jesús Arboleya Cervera

Doctorate in history. Researcher at the Center for National Security Studies; associate of the Center for European Studies; associate of the U.S. History Section of the Faculty of Philosophy and History at the University of Havana; and researcher associated with the Center for U.S. Studies (CESEU) of the University of Havana. He has also researched social anthropology at the University of Havana.

For more than 25 years he worked in the Cuban foreign service, where among his duties he served between 1975-79 on the Social, Humanitarian and Cultural Commission of the United Nations and the NGO Committee of the UN. Between 1979-81 he worked as consul in the Cuban Interests' Section in Washington DC. Since 1990 he has participated in the group dedicated to the émigré community within Cuba's Ministry of Foreign Affairs. He also functioned during this period as a personal adviser to the president of the Cuban Institute for Friendship Among the People.

He has participated in numerous international conferences, among them the General Assemblies of the United Nations in 1972, 1975-79 and 1988.

Introduction

In the summer of 1994, the Caribbean Sea became the scene of the two most dramatic migratory crises in recent years as thousands of would-be immigrants launched homemade rafts in the direction of the United States.

The first wave was the exodus of Haitians which rapidly became out of control and immediately put the spotlight on issues such as racial discrimination, human rights and U.S. national security.

The Clinton administration — which during the electoral campaign had criticized the decision to repatriate Haitian émigrés — now adopted that same repatriation policy, and detained the would-be Haitian immigrants outside U.S. territory for processing. Each case for asylum was then considered individually, since it was felt that, aside from the extreme repression in Haiti, the émigrés were motivated fundamentally by economic reasons.

Guantánamo thus became the repository for these Haitian refugees. This is the U.S. naval base in Cuban territory which the United States has occupied since 1902. Denying the legitimacy of U.S. claims to the site, the Cuban government formally complained to the U.S. government over the decision to house the Haitians in Guantánamo and denounced it in the United Nations. A temporary solution for the problem of the Haitian émigrés was found when, with the U.S. military intervention in

Haiti, it became possible to deport people indiscriminately back to Haiti.

In July 1994, the so-called Cuban rafters crisis added new tensions in the region. It began when dozens of people who wanted to emigrate forced their way into embassies and diplomatic residences in Havana or resorted to seizing planes and ships, causing accidents and creating conflicts in which around 30 potential émigrés and two Cuban policemen lost their lives.

The Cuban government identified the main causes of the illegal wave of émigrés as the tightening by the United States of its blockade of Cuba at a time of economic crisis, the U.S. practice of giving preference to Cubans who emigrated illegally while restricting the number of legal applications granted, and the maintenance of a U.S. propaganda offensive which directly and indirectly urged people to leave Cuba illegally.

On August 24, President Fidel Castro addressed both Cuban and U.S. citizens on television (rebroadcast on CNN), explaining his government's position on these events. In that appearance, he repeated warnings made a few days earlier, saying:

> If the United States doesn't take rapid, effective measures to stop promoting illegal departures from [our] country, we will feel obliged to instruct our border guards to do nothing to stop any vessel that is trying to leave Cuba. We have set forth our position; we aren't opposed to solutions if they are based on sincerity and honesty, if they really seek to solve the problem, if they aren't proffered as a means of deceiving us — but we can't continue to act as border guards for the United States.[1]

Initially, the U.S. government's response was to reaffirm its policy, viewing Fidel Castro's statements as interference in its immigration practice, while further tightening its economic blockade and threatening a naval blockade if Cuba didn't control

---

[1] Fidel Castro, "Comparecencia ante la televisión cubana el 24 de agosto de 1994" [Appearance on Cuban television on August 24, 1994], *Granma*, Havana, August 28, 1994.

the illegal departures. The Cuban government decided to allow all who wanted to leave to do so and to permit boats to come to Cuba's coasts to collect those who wanted to emigrate.

In just a few days around 30,000 Cubans took to the sea in homemade, far from safe rafts and small craft, confident that as had been customary in the past they would be picked up by U.S. ships a few miles offshore and taken to the United States where they would be accepted immediately. But things didn't turn out that way since, for the first time in 35 years, the United States not only did not accept them, but also confined them in virtual concentration camps a few meters from the up-until-then less fortunate Haitian émigrés at Guantánamo. Thus, the Cuban illegal émigrés suddenly found that they had lost their special status under U.S. immigration policy.

The "rafters crisis" — as it became known — polarized U.S. public opinion. On one side were those who called for an even tougher stand against Cuba; on the other, those who (in their majority) advocated a complete review of Washington's Cuba policy, including the lifting of the blockade and normalization of migration.

After a period of tense negotiations, the two governments reached an important agreement on migration. Even though it left essential aspects of the relations between the two countries pending, it was considered a step toward solving the bilateral dispute and, therefore, was welcomed by most governments in the world and praised by the main international mass media.

Nevertheless, the agreement itself shows how the migration question has distorted relations between the two nations and highlights the weight this problem has had in the antagonistic relationship between Cuba and the United States since the 1959 revolution. The U.S. policy on Cuban immigration has been a key element of Washington's intransigent strategy of de-stabilizing the Cuban revolution. This policy has certainly served to strengthen the Cuban counterrevolution and helped the Cuban American rightwing extremists to attain exaggerated influence in U.S. policy on Cuba. The weight of this ultraright "domestic factor" in determining U.S. government policy on

Cuba has been used many times to justify the inertia of that policy and to make demands on the Cuban government which Cubans remaining on the island consider to be a violation of their sovereignty. That element made itself felt again in the "rafters crisis," and was the reason why President Clinton took measures which, in the long run, turned out to be contradictory.

In fact, the myth of the "domestic factor" tends to hide much more complex processes at play in U.S. politics. Underpinning this system is the hegemonic view that, ever since the Monroe Doctrine was formulated in 1823, considers Latin America — and especially Cuba — to be the U.S. backyard. Furthermore, it shows that so far the United States has been unable to draw up a foreign policy in keeping with the reality of the post-Cold War period.

It isn't a matter of the U.S. hegemonic desires having changed; rather, the conditions under which such hegemony can be imposed have changed. Together with the collapse of the European socialist camp, the Doctrine that served as the compass for a bipartisan U.S. foreign policy has been blown to bits. This is why the indecision and ambivalence that are present in the handling of the Cuban issue are, to some extent, the same that can be found in other aspects of Washington's international policy.

This book describes and analyzes the main aspects of the migration dispute between Cuba and the United States and shows that at the heart of this conflict lies the more fundamental issue of the complex dynamics of relations between the big powers and the underdeveloped countries. It reviews the Cuban migration phenomenon as an organic element of U.S. policy based on the philosophy of the Monroe Doctrine that perceives Latin America as part of U.S. patrimony.

Now, when this edition is going to press, it is still to be seen if the migration agreement which was signed between Cuba and the United States on September 9, 1994, constitutes an advance toward a general improvement in relations. Even if its benefits are limited to the issue of migration, it may well establish a new starting point. By no longer welcoming illegal Cuban immigrants the new policy at least eliminates the argument that the émigrés are political asylum seekers and brings this problem much more into line with the growing migratory pressure generated by the universal phenomenon of underdevelopment.

CHAPTER 1

Migration
and U.S. policy toward Cuba

The end of World War II presented the United States with the problem of exercizing its hegemony in a capitalist world that was devastated economically, the colonial system was in a crisis that speeded the development of the national liberation movements in the Third World and a fierce competition with the Soviet Union for military supremacy was initiated. This situation gave rise to the Truman Doctrine, which, based on the strategy of "containing the Soviets," divided the world into two antagonistic blocs and linked the interests of U.S. national security to maintaining a status quo whose slightest alteration constituted a focal point for international tension.

The Cuban case became a typical example of the extreme application of that philosophy. The problem of Cuba's dependent relationship with the United States existed long before the emergence of the Soviet Union. By the middle of the last century, the United States had already supplanted Spain as the dominant power in the Cuban economy. Its political control was asserted with the U.S. intervention in Cuba's 1898 War of Independence, its occupation of the island until 1902 and its imposition and maintenance of a neocolonial regime from then on.

The struggle against this neocolonial dependence left its mark on the Cuban political process during the first half of the 20th century and was a direct factor behind the 1959 revolution. Probably no other international event had such a marked impact on the economic, political and ideological foundations of U.S. hegemony. Cuba was a small, Third World country where the United States had first launched its neocolonial project and which it considered its safest domain.

That is why, in March 1960, President Eisenhower readily approved the plans for overthrowing the Cuban revolution. Originally, the United States had thought of applying the same methods it had used in 1954 against the nationalist upsurge in Guatemala, and to this end had already activated some of the CIA agents who had participated in the Guatemalan operation.[2] Popular support for the Cuban process, however, showed that the counterrevolution didn't have much chance of overthrowing the revolutionary government by itself or surviving inside the country, which made it necessary to quickly change those plans. It was therefore decided to organize the main counter-revolutionary forces outside the country and to work toward creating the conditions for direct intervention by the United States. Those were the conceptual premises for the Bay of Pigs invasion in 1961.

Cuba's later alliance with the socialist camp — which was probably inevitable, in view of the geopolitical and ideological conditions in which the Cuban revolution had to develop — added an important element to the Cuba-U.S. dispute. However, this was never its main cause, as shown by the fact that 30 years later, when the socialist camp had been dismantled, the Soviet Union had disappeared and the historical period of the Cold War was supposedly a thing of the past, the premises determining U.S. policy toward Cuba have not changed.

---

[2] Peter Wyden, *Bay of Pigs: The untold story*, 24-25.

Destabilizing role of the Cuban emigration

The plans of the United States required the creation of powerful stimuli for Cuban emigration. That emigration was to serve as a social base for the counterrevolution and also helped to drain the country of its human capital, which was indispensable for the country's socioeconomic development. It was also to be used to stigmatize the Cuban political project and detract from its popular support with a view to neutralizing its influence in Latin America. That is why, just a few hours after it was decided to implement the plans already mentioned, Eisenhower addressed the U.S. Congress to seek its support for a strategy for publicizing and assisting the Cuban émigrés.[3]

The counterrevolutionary function that the United States assigned to the Cuban émigrés gave them a singular political significance that differentiated them from all other Latin American immigrants and from the many Cubans who had gone to the United State prior to the triumph of the revolution. Even though, on the sociological level, the individual motivation for emigrating was essentially economic, those Cubans who decided to emigrate did so aware of this political context. Their position as political refugees was reinforced by the extent to which they received direct and indirect benefits, and it was a prerequisite for their inclusion in the community of Cuban émigrés.

The emigration of its citizens is, first of all, to be understood in the context of Cuban society. It was in that social dynamic that the conflicts, dissatisfactions and aspirations arose that stimulated the desire to seek new horizons. In this regard, I would like to point out that this trend was nourished, given shape and inspired in the context of the conflict between the two countries — which gave the issue its political edge.

Whereas the Cuban migratory problem also reflected the natural flow of people from less developed countries to more developed ones — and the trend to emigrate to the United States has been present in Cuban society for nearly two centuries — the impact of the Cuban revolution altered its dynamic and its

---

[3] Félix R. Masud-Piloto, *With open arms*, 34.

composition. The process of transformation of Cuban society which started in 1959 inevitably alienated a relatively important segment of the population, and emigration became one of the ways — perhaps the most obvious one — in which that dissatisfaction was expressed.

However, considering only the possible motives of each individual is, in itself, a methodological approximation which makes it difficult to understand the problem. The act of emigrating is generally a complex, traumatic decision which has many causes, and it reflects to some extent the individual's dissatisfaction with their situation or with what they expect to get out of life. In such a framework it is nearly impossible to discern where the economic influence ends and where the political — or even psychological — one begins.

There have been cases of people who have been forced to emigrate from their countries as a result of the political persecution to which they have been subjected; that is the criteria behind the definition of a "political refugee," as accepted by the Convention Relating to the Status of Refugees approved by the United Nations in 1949. Although there are some exceptions, from that perspective Cuban emigration doesn't have a political nature, since the vast majority of those people haven't left the country because they were persecuted for their political ideas. Many of them — especially in the most recent generations of émigrés — have left without any substantial conflicts with the revolutionary process. But, even if this weren't so, political nonconformity doesn't determine status as a political refugee. There must also be a certain level of persecution that makes life in their own country impossible for the individual concerned, and this has not been the case in Cuba.

Nevertheless, Cuban migration since the 1959 revolution has been essentially political, because political factors made it possible and molded its characteristics. As U.S. sociologist Robert Bach states, the political or economic nature of a given migration should be analyzed on the basis of the form it assumes and the degree to which it is orchestrated by the governments involved.[4]

U.S. immigration policy with regard to Cuba has been applied in violation of the criteria normally accepted in international practice. For example, the concept of "political refugee" has been applied to Cuban émigrés indiscriminately. Early on the criteria used were those contained in the Walter-McCarran Act, which the U.S. Congress passed in 1952 to stimulate emigration from the European socialist countries in the context of heightened Cold War tensions. That practice didn't change even when, in 1969, the United States signed the protocol of the UN Convention Relating to the Status of Refugees, or when the Refugee Act of 1980 adopted the UN's criteria.[5]

Washington's strategy was based on the expectation that the "Cuban problem" would develop rapidly, and therefore transitory in nature. This strategy was later to be complicated when the Cuban revolution managed to survive the pressures that were exerted against it, and the settling of Cuban émigrés in the United States became considered a lifetime choice. This policy has been affected by the pressures imposed by the domestic debate on immigration to the United States. Therefore, not all groups of Cuban émigrés have received equal treatment on entering and settling in that country.

The first generation of émigrés
The first émigrés included most of those who might best be considered "political exiles," since in many cases they were key figures in the Batista dictatorship who fled to the United States and other countries to escape revolutionary justice. Later on, most of the Cuban oligarchy joined them, followed soon by the rest of the more privileged sectors in the country, including a considerable proportion of Cuba's professionals and most highly skilled technicians.

---

[4] Robert Bach, *The Cuban exodus: Political and economic motivations*, 110.
[5] For more information in this regard, see the books I have cited by U.S. sociologists Félix R. Masud-Piloto and Robert Bach.

From the quantitative point of view, 31 percent of that emigration consisted of managers, technicians and professionals, and 33 percent were bureaucrats and businessmen. In Cuba they constituted 9.2 and 13.7 percent of the total workforce according to the 1953 census. But the figures comparing the educational level of those émigrés with that of Cuban society as a whole at the time are even more indicative: 36 percent of the émigrés were high school graduates, while only 4 percent of the total population had attained that educational level. Moreover, only 4 percent of the émigrés had less than a fourth-grade education, while 52 percent of all Cubans were in that group.[6]

There haven't been many revolutionary processes like that of Cuba in which the accelerated and comprehensive emigration occurred of a social group that constituted the dominant political-economic bloc in Cuban neocolonial society. Under the auspices of the United States, a significant proportion of those first émigrés joined the counterrevolution and settled in conditions that were favorable enough for them to recover, to some extent, their former position and become the prevailing sector in the Cuban community in the United States.

In that period, between the 1959 revolution and October 1962, around 200,000 people emigrated. In line with the strategy described above, the United States gave them top visa priority. It even authorized individuals and entities, such as the Catholic Church, to grant visa waivers — created for cases of extreme emergency — when it broke off diplomatic relations with Cuba in January 1961.

It was at this time that the CIA, again with the support of the Catholic Church, implemented Operation Peter Pan, which consisted of promoting — by spreading rumors that the revolutionary government would do away with patria potestas (parental rights) — the emigration of children unaccompanied by their parents. Those children subsequently found themselves interned in children's camps or with U.S. families as their guardians. Two hundred children emigrated in those conditions

---

[6] Bach, *The Cuban exodus*, 112.

every week in 1961,[7] and it is estimated that a total of around 14,000 left in this way.[8]

From the point of view of assistance, the most important decision that was made at that time was the creation of the Cuban Refugee Program in February 1961. Originally conceived as an extension of the 1956 assistance to and relocation of Hungarian refugees in the United States, it was also designed with a view to providing a temporary solution for the problem of how to get the Cuban émigrés to settle outside the state of Florida until they could go back to Cuba. Its initial cost was estimated at around $4 million, but it continued to exist up until 1975 and cost more than $1 million a year, making it the most extensive and expensive such program ever in the United States.[9]

The failure of the 1961 Bay or Pigs invasion and the aftermath of the 1962 October Missile Crisis clearly changed the U.S. view of the durability of the Cuban revolution — and therefore the way the problem of the Cuban émigrés should be handled. Although the Migration and Refugee Assistance Act — by virtue of which most of the Cuban immigrants were granted the status of "political refugee" — had been passed in early 1962, President Kennedy suspended direct flights between the United States and Cuba by the end of the year, leaving tens of thousands of people who hoped to emigrate stranded in Cuba. This included a large number of parents whose children were already in the United States.

Their only alternative was to get visas and the money for traveling to a third country and from there request entry to the United States under conditions similar to those of other potential immigrants, as part of the country quotas set by U.S. law. However, those who emigrated from Cuba illegally and entered the United States without complying with any of those

---

[7] Masud-Piloto, *With open arms*, 39-40.

[8] Gail Epstein, "Beneficiarios del proyecto Pedro Pan ofrecen homenaje a su benefactora" [Beneficiaries of the Peter Pan Project render homage to their benefactor], *El Nuevo Herald*, June 27, 1993.

[9] Masud-Piloto, *With open arms*, 53.

requirements were given preferential treatment and immediately granted the status of "political refugee."

This situation created a tremendous incentive for the illegal emigration by Cubans — which reached one of the highest levels, when around 30,000 people emigrated that way between 1962 and 1965.[10] The Cuban government's response to the pressure of that illegal migratory flow in late 1965 was to open a marina in the port of Camarioca, in the northwestern part of the island, to which those émigrés who wanted to pick up their relatives and take them to the United States could come freely with the required safety precautions.

In October and November that year, around 2,700 people emigrated through Camarioca,[11] creating a situation which forced the United States to sign a Memorandum of Understanding in December 1965. This was the first document in which the two governments established an agreement for handling the emigration in an organized way.

In the Memorandum of Understanding, the U.S. government pledged to transport between 3,000 and 4,000 Cubans a month to the United States, giving priority to those with close relatives in that country. The Cuban government placed tight restrictions on the departure of people considered indispensable to the economy and young men of military age, those between 15 and 26 years of age.[12]

Around 250,000 people emigrated to the United States in this way during the eight years the agreement was in effect.[13] Ninety percent of them had relatives there, so the process of family reunification was quite extensive, having a considerable impact on the demographic shape of the Cuban émigré community and its subsequent relations with Cuba.[14]

---

[10] Mercedes Arce, et al. *La emigración en Cuba, 1959-1990* [Emigration in Cuba, 1959-90], 5.

[11] Arce, *La emigración*, 5.

[12] Masud-Piloto, *With open arms*, 62.

[13] Masud-Piloto, *With open arms*, 68.

[14] Bach, *The Cuban exodus*, 113.

However, those agreements weren't the result of any improvement in the relations between the two countries. Even though those who emigrated did so completely voluntarily, under a bilateral agreement through normal immigration procedures and with adequate means of transportation, they continued to be considered "political refugees." The airlift was dubbed "Freedom Flights," and no distinction was made between legal and illegal immigration. During that period, around 10,500 Cubans entered U.S. territory illegally, and they were given the same treatment as before.[15]

As a result of the complete review of U.S. immigration policy that took place in 1965 in order to cut the costs of the Cuban Refugee Program and make it legal for those immigrants to remain in the United States on a permanent basis, the Johnson administration approved the Cuban Adjustment Act in 1966, granting political asylum to all Cuban immigrants. It also simplified the process and shortened the time established by law for their obtaining residential status and U.S. citizenship.

As long as the Cuban Refugee Program remained in effect, that law had a limited impact on the status of Cuban immigrants, since the program offered unprecedented advantages. However, when the program was canceled in 1975, the law facilitated the speedy naturalization of those immigrants and, above all, set a legal precedent that in itself stimulated later illegal immigration. From that moment on, every Cuban who reached U.S. soil was welcomed as a political refugee and, in two years, would obtain residential status in the United States. Doris Meissner, Commissioner of the U.S. Naturalization and Immigration Service, described that law as a national shame because of its discriminatory nature against other immigrants and the political manipulation implicit in its application. She urged that it be eliminated on the understanding that the adjustments contained

---

[15] Arce, *La emigración*, 6.

in the 1980 immigration law made it unnecessary to make any exceptions for the Cubans.[16]

End of the first generation of émigrés

In 1973, President Nixon decided to put an end to the airlift and to suspend the agreements that had given rise to it, pushing the migratory problem between the two countries back to where it had been in 1965. It may be said that this marked the end of the first phase of emigration after the revolution. By then, around 630,000 Cubans had settled in the United States, and even though all strata of Cuban society were represented, it is clear that the majority was from the upper echelons of the pre-revolutionary social scale, especially the bourgeoisie and the sectors of the middle class that had benefited most from the previous regime.

The links between the first generation of émigrés and Cuban society on the island tended to weaken as entire families were reunited abroad. Personal contact between those who had left and those who had stayed was practically nonexistent up until 1979, while the revolution transformed the deeply rooted values and cultural and ideological models of Cuban society.

The profound transformation of the Cuban social structure changed the political, ideological and cultural frames of reference of the first wave of émigrés, so their conflict with the revolution became related not only to the recovery of the status, property and privileges they had lost in Cuba, but also to a way of life and individual values that were no longer the reality of the new Cuban society. That conflict was evident in the composition and goals of the counterrevolutionary movement and largely explains the extreme polarization between the revolution and the counter-revolution in Cuba.

In 1973, a historical period came to an end. This was the period in which U.S. policy on Cuba was blatantly inter-ventionist, sponsoring very aggressive forms of counter-revolutionary activity and encouraging the emigration of a

---

[16] Cinthia Coro, "Cambio de la política deja en un limbo la Ley de Ajuste" [Change in policy leaves the Adjustment Act in limbo], *El Nuevo Herald*, August 20, 1994.

segment of Cuban society that, without being homogeneous, clearly represented the economic, political, social and ideological structures that served as the base for the neocolonial republic.

This gave rise to very marked class differences between the émigrés abroad and Cuban society on the island, with the consequent alienation of the political émigré groups from national life as they adopted goals that had been left behind in Cuba or represented interests that no longer corresponded to those of the majority of the population. This is why, no matter what the motives, most of those who left — especially those who left Cuba after 1980 — reflected another social reality, and their conflict with the revolution lacked the class character of the earlier groups of émigrés.

The first wave of émigrés retained very close family ties and they benefited the most from the U.S. government's preferential immigration policy. Because of the role they had played in neocolonial society, they were best prepared for integration and their later role in the extension of trade and investments between southern Florida and Latin America. They were also the group that benefited the most from the investments the CIA made, especially in Miami, for its secret war against Cuba.

Members of that generation participated extensively in counterrevolutionary activities, especially in the 1960s, and this helped to forge the political links that gave them status and brought them additional economic benefits. In addition, the training which many of them were given by the CIA and the links that counterrevolutionary activities generated with Latin American governments as well as military and paramilitary groups, led many émigrés to direct involvement in the traffic in drugs — one of the main sources of the capital with which the Cuban American elite reestablished itself in the United States.

By 1980, the first generation of Cuban émigrés had been integrated into U.S. society to such an extent that it was already possible to speak of a category of Cuban Americans in the social structure. The complexity of the process of their social integration in a multinational and multi-ethnic society such as the United States is a topic that goes beyond the limits of this work. Suffice it to say, therefore, that it was a process that was consolidated when the immigrants began to consider themselves as U.S. citizens and were accepted as such by the rest of society on the basis of the economic relations which they, as a minority group, established within the ruling social structure.

The social integration of the Cuban émigrés and the corresponding consolidation of a Cuban American community in the United States has had political, legal and cultural consequences of great importance for the Cuban nation. One particular feature is the extraterritorial expression of Cuban culture, a new phenomenon for the history of a nation which thus far had seen its culture and national identity arise and develop almost exclusively within its national boundaries.

This new reality has become an important factor in stimulating emigration, for it generates a process of family reunification, tends to develop very close cultural contacts and is a source of expectations of a better standard of living for certain segments of the population who, at one time or another, are prepared to face the challenge of emigration.

At first, the new groups of immigrants in the United States tended to create a subculture which met their needs for self-identification and created mechanisms of collective defense. For the Cubans, that environment was created in Miami, an enclave that has been exploited consciously as an archetype for the aspirations of Latin American development and as a permanent spur to emigration from Cuba.[17]

The Cuban American enclave in Miami
Around 50 percent of the Cubans residing in the United States live in Dade County, a region consisting of 28 municipalities in

---

[17] The phenomenon of social integration, which is also defined as assimilation or transculturation, depending on the criteria of the authors, has been extensively studied by historians, sociologists and anthropologists. In the case of the Cuban community in the United States, it has been discussed by researchers such as Portes, Bach, Lisandro Pérez, Urriarte, Pérez-Stable and Rumbaut, in most cases from a comparative demographic perspective. In Cuba, it has been taken up in the doctoral theses of Mercedes Arce and the author of this book.

the southernmost part of Florida that is generally referred to as Miami.[18]

This region has a population of over 2 million, 30 percent of whom are of Cuban origin. Therefore, this is where what has come to be known as Miami's "Cuban American enclave" emerged. This enclave has become the economic, political and social epicenter of the Cuban community living in the United States, and serves as a cultural model also for Cuban Americans who live outside the region.

Since 1959, Miami has been one of the fastest growing cities in the United States. This process was influenced by external and internal factors that molded a specific economic, political and social context which determined how it was possible for the Cubans in the United States to attain such relative success.

The Cuban immigrants' massive arrival in southern Florida initially caused an increase in unemployment, a drop in wages and a deterioration in the local social welfare programs. However, the government plans already mentioned, such as the Cuban Refugee Program, and the investments that were made to turn the region into a CIA base of operations, put the area's economy on a steady keel.

The arrival of growing numbers of Cuban immigrants also coincided with an increase in U.S. investments in the most productive spheres of the Latin American economy and with renewed interest in the region that wasn't unrelated to the triumph of the Cuban revolution. This meant increased job opportunities for many Cuban immigrants who, in addition to having the required language skills and cultural links, had the advantage of having had earlier ties with the U.S. companies and the confidence that flowed from their political experience.

Miami's economy is primarily dependent on foreign trade, tourism and services for Latin American capital and U.S. investors interested in this area. Around 200 multinational corporations have offices there, 50 percent of the State of Florida's foreign trade is generated in the region, and 90 percent

---

[18] In speaking of Dade County and its environs, I also use the name Miami. When referring to the municipality, I specify that this is the case.

of U.S. trade with Latin America goes through Miami. Those businesses had an income of $25.6 billion in 1993.[19]

According to data provided by Miami's Center for Hemispheric Studies, around $96 billion was deposited in the city's banking system in 1986. Around $25 billion of that sum came from abroad, most of it private capital expatriated from Latin America. The port of Miami makes a profit of around $6 billion a year and Miami's airport is the second most important in the country. Tourism contributes around $7 billion a year.[20]

Seventy percent of the cocaine and marijuana consumed in the United States — an estimated $40 to $80 billion worth a year — enters the country through this region. This greatly influences the economy and the legal and political functioning of society, turning southern Florida into one of the regions with the highest indices of crime and violence in the United States.[21]

Thus, Miami has become the hub of U.S. trade relations with Latin America, an important international financial center, one of the main ports of entry for drugs and key center of Hispanic life.

In spite of the fact that Cuban Americans constitute only 4.8 percent of the Hispanic population in the United States, close to a third of the largest Hispanic companies are based in the area, including the main offices of two of the three Hispanic television networks. Miami is one of the largest U.S. cities where Hispanics constitute the majority of the population.[22]

The role of Cuban Americans in U.S. relations with Latin America has developed as Miami became the political center of monitoring developments in Latin America and the logistics base

---

[19] These data have been taken from several articles which appeared in the U.S. press, especially "Miami's Cubans," by Carlos Arboleya, which was published in the May 17, 1985, edition of *Diario de las Américas*; several articles published in the May 5, 1986, edition of *The Miami Herald*; and the special issue of *Time* magazine on migration — "The new face of America," autumn 1993.

[20] Cathy Booth, "Miami," *Time*, autumn 1993.

[21] Penny Lernoux, "The golden gateway of drugs: the Miami connection," *The Nation*, February 18, 1984.

[22] Booth, *Time*.

for counterinsurgency and counterrevolutionary plans in the continent.

The interrelationship of all these elements affected the process of integration of the Cuban émigrés into U.S. society and consolidated a clearly differentiated class structure within the enclave, in which the most conservative ideological currents and a climate of extreme political intolerance prevail. It is this intolerance which has been denounced by such institutions as Americas Watch and the American Civil Liberties Union. Moreover, terrorism has more impunity in the enclave than anywhere else in the United States.

The socio-economic structure of the community is difficult to determine. However, about 1 percent constitutes the ruling group of businessmen and 8 percent smaller business interests. An important sector of administrative officials and professionals accounts for less than 30 percent of the total, while close to 60 percent are wage workers, 40 percent of whom are among the worst paid in the region. Five to 10 percent of the population of working age is unemployed, and an undetermined number are engaged in marginal and criminal activities.[23]

According to the main economic indices Miami's Cuban American community is at a point halfway between the U.S. social average and the Hispanic and black groups, which are the ones least favored by the system. On this basis, some specialists in the United States consider that, in fact, only 20 percent have achieved the level of economic success which some have presented as reflecting the entire community.[24]

The standard of living in the United States is higher than that in Cuba, so the implicit attraction of greater economic development will inevitably form part of the desire to migrate.

---

[23] My figures are based on data from *Cubans in the changing economy of Miami* by Marifeli Pérez-Stable and Miran Urriarte; *Immigrant America* by Alejandro Portes and Rubén Rumbaut; *General overview of the Cuban influx since 1959* by Antonio Jorge and Raúl Moncarz; and *El potencial económico de las empresas pertenecientes a cubano-americanos en EE.UU.* [Economic potential of the companies belonging to Cuban Americans in the United States] by Roxana Brizuela and Luis Fernández-Tabío.

[24] Pérez-Stable and Urriarte, 15.

But even taking this objective economic reality into account, the significant social imbalances that exist within the Cuban American community itself and the inevitable difficulties involved in the experience of migration are frequently overlooked. The picture of Miami's Cuban American enclave has been "sold" to Cubans for ideological and political purposes, exaggerating the relative success of the Cuban émigrés in the United States and creating false expectations among those wanting to emigrate.

CHAPTER 2

The second wave of émigrés

Between 1973 and 1979, another 50,000 Cubans emigrated — a significant drop in the migratory flow as a result of the suspension of the agreements and because the Cuban economy was healthier.[25] This was also a period of reduced tension between Cuba and the United States; counterrevolutionary activities decreased considerably; while the Nixon and Ford administrations, in the spirit of the policy of détente, initiated discreet contacts with the Cuban government.[26] However, these contacts were broken off when the consensus on the policy toward the Soviet Union deteriorated, the Republicans were weakened by the Watergate scandal, and new conflicts appeared between Cuba and the United States over matters related to Puerto Rico's status and the war in Angola. Furthermore, the 1976 election forced Gerald Ford to shift to the right to woo the conservative vote.

The Carter administration, however, renewed the process of improving relations with considerable energy, and by the end of Carter's first year in office the ban on U.S. citizens' travel to Cuba had been lifted, agreements had been signed allowing

---

[25] Masud-Piloto, *With open arms*, 3.
[26] A chronology of this little-publicized process can be found in *United States-Cuba détente: The 1974-75 initiative and Angolan intervention*, published by the National Security Archives in 1993.

Cubans to fish in U.S. jurisdictional waters, the agreements on the hijacking of planes and ships were renewed, and diplomatic offices had been opened in Havana and Washington (mirroring the rapprochement between the United States and China). In spite of differences over many issues, there was a significant increase in diplomatic, academic and cultural exchanges between the two countries, and most signs pointed to the normalization of relations.

That climate made it easier for the Cuban government to take some key steps in its policy on emigration, the most important of them being the calling for a dialogue in late 1978 with representatives of the Cuban community abroad.

The 1978 dialogue

President Fidel Castro's call for the dialogue defined what, from the Cuban point of view, had made it possible to take this step: the revolution had been consolidated, changes in U.S. policy toward Cuba had taken place, and a decline in hostility could be noted in the émigré community.[27]

As a result of that meeting, Cuba decided to free over 3,000 political prisoners and negotiated with the United States to arrange for their transfer to that country, along with their relatives and around 600 former prisoners who were waiting to emigrate there. It also agreed to allow those émigrés who wanted to visit Cuba to do so. In 1979, some 100,000 of them took up the offer.[28]

Unquestionably, this meant a basic change in the Cuban government's relations with the émigrés, but it wasn't easy for either of the two sides from the political point of view. The Cuban American ultrarightists in Miami reacted to the dialogue and the improvement in relations between Cuba and the United

---

[27] Fidel Castro, *Entrevista con periodistas que escriben para la comunidad cubana en el exterior, el 6 de setiembre de 1978* [Interview with journalists who write for the Cuban community abroad, September 6, 1978].

[28] For more details on this meeting and its results, see *Las corrientes políticas en la comunidad de origen cubano en los Estados Unidos* [Political currents in the Cuban community in the United States], doctoral thesis by this author.

States with a wave of terrorism of unprecedented scope in U.S. territory. Most of the émigrés were pleased at the possibility of traveling to Cuba, which both enraged the extreme right and destroyed all the myths about the nature of the émigrés and their commitment to the counterrevolutionary cause. Nevertheless, this shouldn't be interpreted as an evolution toward a new ideological point of view or as a significant increase in support for the revolution in the community. It was simply a necessary social and psychological adjustment that overcame the pressure of the most extremist groups. However, it constituted a very important step, in view of the political intransigence which prevailed in the émigré community.

The meeting with the émigrés was traumatic for Cuban society, as well. Emigration had had a political significance that polarized families and made the decision to remain in Cuba an expression of patriotism. The role the émigrés played in counterrevolutionary activities helped strengthen this conviction, and links with relatives abroad were almost considered an ideological weakness that kept many people from belonging to the more militant and selective organizations, such as the Communist Party and the Union of Young Communists.

Moreover, the émigrés returned to Cuba boasting of the supposed economic success they had achieved in the United States, enhancing the Miami model and offering false guarantees of support for those who wanted to emigrate — considering that the absence of a migration agreement between the two countries made it highly unlikely that the others could leave the country. This situation undermined those sectors that were most closely allied to the revolution and spurred others who hadn't previously considered leaving to think of doing so.

In 1979, Cuba's relations with the United States changed dramatically, due to the weakness of the Carter administration and to the growing weight of a conservative offensive that swung the U.S. political pendulum decisively to the right, revitalizing the anti-Cuba forces.

The deterioration in Cuba's relations with the United States, the build-up of numbers of potential emigrants as a result of the suspension of the normal migratory flow for seven years and the expectations that had been encouraged through links with the émigrés, once again stimulated illegal emigration at the end of the decade and influenced the "Mariel crisis" in 1980.

Mariel

The first manifestations of this crisis were an increase in seizures of ships and planes and, more serious, breaking into several Latin American embassies by individuals in the hope that they could obtain visas for emigration to the United States through third countries.

The Cuban government refused to accept that practice, since those individuals weren't being persecuted for political reasons and there was no reason for granting them the right of asylum. Moreover, Cuba agreed that those who wanted to emigrate should do so freely to any country that would accept them; but, for the safety of the embassies, it couldn't allow a precedent to be established that gave preference to those who entered them by means of force.

Early in 1980, 12 individuals forced their way into the Peruvian embassy. Negotiations were entered into with the ambassador concerning their voluntary departure from the embassy, Cuba providing guarantees that it would allow them to emigrate to Peru later on if that government accepted them. An agreement that was apparently satisfactory to both parties was reached. The ambassador explained his position to the Cuban press and the 12 returned to their homes, waiting for Peruvian visas. Inexplicably, however, the Peruvian government reneged on the agreement a few days later and ordered the ambassador to again give the 12 asylum in the embassy. The Cuban government interpreted this as a flagrant act of provocation. The situation that was created immediately led other people to force their way into embassies: in March 1980, there were 25 in the Peruvian embassy, 15 in the Venezuelan embassy and one in the Argentine embassy.[29]

---

[29] Masud-Piloto, *With open arms*, 70.

On April 1, a new attempt was made to break into the Peruvian embassy and one of the Cuban guards was killed. The Cuban government, citing the lack of cooperation shown by the Peruvian authorities, decided to withdraw its protection from that embassy and to allow anybody who wanted to emigrate to that country to enter the embassy's grounds. In less than 72 hours, around 10,000 people did so.

In the United States, the massive crowd in the Peruvian embassy was interpreted as a rebellion against the Cuban revolution and Washington encouraged it by offering guarantees to those who took such actions. The Organization of American States promoted the idea of creating camps for Cuban refugees in various Latin American countries and projects of that kind were attempted in Peru and Costa Rica.

Cuba's response to those pressures was to announce that nobody else could enter the grounds of the Peruvian embassy and to maintain its position that it would not authorize anyone who forced their way into another embassy to leave the country. However, it said that everyone who wanted to emigrate could do so. The port of Mariel, in the northwestern part of the country, was readied to receive vessels from the United States that would come to Cuba to pick up potential emigrants — this time, with the condition that the vessels wouldn't take just the relatives of those who sent them, but would also take other people who wanted to leave the country but didn't have the means for doing so.

At first, the Cuban community in the United States was glad to take up the offer, and hundreds of vessels immediately set out. For its part, the U.S. government maintained its traditional stance at first, describing the émigrés as political dissidents. Carter himself declared that his administration would continue to "provide an open heart and open arms for the tens of thousands of refugees seeking freedom from Communist domination."[30]

---

[30] Masud-Piloto, *With open arms,* 83.

The avalanche of the more than 125,000 émigrés who left via Mariel rapidly overwhelmed the U.S. immigration system and meant the new Cuban immigrants were treated very differently from their predecessors. Those who left through Mariel weren't granted automatic political asylum or privileged social assistance. To the contrary, they found themselves publicly rejected and interned in virtual concentration camps and prisons, where some of them still remain. At the end of 1980, they were included in the general law on refugees that had been passed that year. The problem of their residential status wasn't solved until 1984 when, in the context of a review of the migration laws and the negotiations that were being held with Cuba, the Reagan administration agreed to have the Cuban Adjustment Act of 1966 applied to them.

The conditions for Cuban immigrants' settling and integrating into U.S. society from then on has, therefore, been very different from those of the earlier groups. Within the community itself they have been discriminated against on the basis of their social origin and race, since for the first time the immigrants included a large number of blacks and mulattos. Even though their cultural impact has been considerable, they have been placed at a disadvantage in the social hierarchy of the Cuban American enclave and therefore have less political representation.

U.S. propaganda on the Mariel crisis was very intense, and media coverage in the capitalist countries generally denounced Cuba severely. Cuba's international image and relations with other countries were seriously damaged as a result.

On the island, this was viewed as an act of aggression, and the people mobilized to reaffirm the revolutionary commitment of the majority. Positions on the issue of migration were polarized once again. Those who had opposed the dialogue and the reestablishment of relations with the Cuban community abroad felt vindicated, and the new émigrés were rejected strongly, with a tendency to stereotype them as antisocial elements and undesirables.

Both the Cuban and the U.S. press emphasized the supposed criminal and antisocial nature of that migratory wave. In fact, according to figures given by U.S. specialists, although 16 percent of those who left Cuba via Mariel had served prison terms in Cuba, in most of those cases it was for having attempted to leave illegally or for having engaged in economic activities that were illegal in Cuba at the time but have been common practice in the United States and any other capitalist country.[31] However, the studies on this subject have ignored one thing: the fact that, paradoxically, the socioeconomic characteristics of those who left through Mariel reflected, to a great extent, the social advances that Cuban society had made by that time. Seventy-four percent of them had worked before emigrating; their average educational level was similar to that of the Cuban community in the United States; and 9 percent were professionals — a figure that was larger than for any previous group of Cuban émigrés.[32]

Unlike the trend manifested in the first generation of émigrés, only 40 percent of those who emigrated in 1980 had relatives in the United States, so this group's links with Cuban society are closer, and the problem of divided families was repeated.[33] Their cultural contact had been more recent, too, and this group's participation in counterrevolutionary activities has been much more limited.

As a result, the emigration subsequent to 1979 added a new heterogeneous element to the social character and class polarization in the Cuban American community. Moreover, fear of massive, uncontrolled immigration changed the basis of U.S. public support for the emigration: its supposed exceptional nature. This meant that, from then on, more selective policies would be applied in the legal immigration of Cubans.

However, this didn't prevent the hardening of U.S. policy toward Cuba (which came about with the Reagan presidency), or end the practice of giving preference to those who arrived in the United States by illegal means. Once again the émigrés were

---

[31] Bach, *The Cuban exodus*, 116.
[32] Bach, *The Cuban exodus*, 116.
[33] Masud-Piloto, *With open arms*, 97.

assigned a major counterrevolutionary role — which undermined the climate of détente that had been achieved with the 1978 dialogue.

Role of the Cuban American right in U.S. policy on Cuba

Reagan's victory was interpreted as a mandate for the New Right to change the models of U.S. domestic and foreign policy. To a large extent, the foreign projection of conservative policy constituted a distancing from the relative moderation with which the containment theory had been applied since the Vietnam War, which meant an increase in the arms race, plans for reversing the advances of Third World nationalist movements and efforts to destabilize the socialist camp.

Cuba was considered the stimulus to the revolutionary movement in Latin America, so a declared anti-Cuban objective was evident in the U.S. invasion of Grenada, its "secret war" against the Sandinista government and U.S. counterinsurgency activities in El Salvador. The possibility of a direct invasion of Cuba by U.S. troops couldn't be ruled out.

Counterrevolutionary activities were reorganized, but this time the conservative Cuban American groups were given a bigger role in designing and implementing U.S. policy on Cuba, in line with the advances the Cuban immigrants had made in their integration into U.S. society.

Thus, the Cuban American ultraright became part of a much more all-encompassing effort, in coincidence with the interests and aspirations of the most conservative groups in U.S. society, which in that period managed to establish their political predominance.

At that point, the Cuban American National Foundation was created. It was a project conceived of, designed and organized by some of the main functionaries in the Reagan administration in the spirit of the President's National Security Directive 17 — which among other things stated that its purpose was to promote public pressure against Cuba by using the Cuban community in the United States.[34] When this plan was drawn up, Richard Allen, who was National Security Adviser at the time, took personal charge of selecting the individuals who were to create the organization and giving them his ideas along with a pledge of support from the government.[35]

Key figures joining the organization were a group of conservative Cuban American intellectuals linked to the think tanks and political groups of the New Right in Washington; another small group of Cuban American politicians affiliated with the Republican Party; and, most significant of all, an ultra-right sector of the Cuban American business interests in Miami. This Miami group had historically been linked to the counterrevolution and to the CIA's plans against Cuba, and was then struggling to get a foothold in local politics so it could consolidate and extend its businesses in the area.[36]

The purpose of Reagan's policy was precisely to turn the Cuban problem into a domestic matter, in order to neutralize the support given during the Carter administration to the current that advocated a change in U.S. policy on Cuba. In this, they counted on the pressure that a segment of U.S. voters could bring to bear. In exchange for that service the Cuban American ultraright received political and material support that enabled it to enter local politics, boost its national impact — another indirect source of personal benefits — and get the nearest thing to a stranglehold on the political life of the Cuban American community.

The Cuban American National Foundation was never representative of the entire community, even though it tries to

---

[34] María Teresa Miyar, *La comunidad cubana y el tema de las relaciones Cuba-EE.UU* [The Cuban community and the topic of Cuba-U.S. relations], 26.

[35] Gaeton Fonzi, "Who is Jorge Mas Canosa?," *Esquire*, January 1993, 121.

[36] For more details on the composition, functioning and purposes of this and other counterrevolutionary organizations created during the neoconservative offensive, see the author's article, "Las nuevas vertientes de la contrarrevolución cubana: una imagen fabricada para Europa" [New expressions of the Cuban counterrevolution: An image made for Europe], in *Revista de Estudios Europeos*, published by the European Study Center, Vol. VI, No. 25-26, 122-132.

present itself as such. What it does reflect is the degree of domination that the ultraright sector of Cuban American businessmen has managed to impose on the rest of the community. That control is based on the predominantly conservative ideology of Cuban émigrés and on the marginal benefits that the new counterrevolutionary upsurge has brought to a part of the community. That control has also been exercised through the application of all kinds of coercive measures against those who have dared to defy it.

The weight of the ultraright in the political orientation of the Cuban American community influenced the debate on the priority and treatment that should be given to the problem of relations with the island, increasing the gap between those who advocated that such relations be maintained and those who sought to subordinate that issue to the larger one of the blockade policy and the isolation of Cuba.

In spite of the control that the first émigrés had already established over the political, social and cultural life of the Cuban American community, a 1991 poll conducted by Florida International University showed that 56 percent of Cuban Americans were in favor of negotiations on migration and family exchanges, showing a sustained trend in favor of the solution of those problems, no matter the form in which such an arrangement might be achieved.[37]

The 1984 migration agreement

The Mariel émigrés created a problem for the U.S. government: that of the "excludables" — thousands of people who, according to immigration criteria, didn't qualify to remain in the United States, either because of their criminal record in Cuba or because of law violations committed after arriving in the United States. The solution found for those cases was to keep them in prison, even after they had served their terms — placing them in a legal

---

[37] Guillermo Grenier, et al. *Views on policy options toward Cuba held by Cuban American residents of Dade County, Fla.: The results of the second 1991 poll.*

limbo that was severely criticized in legal circles and by some U.S. public commentators.

In addition, it was stated that the Cubans had unilaterally solved the "Mariel crisis" and that there was no way of regulating emigration from Cuba within the framework of the immigration problem in the United States — a priority item on the Republican conservatives' agenda.

Therefore, in spite of the exacerbation of tension between the two countries, the United States proposed in 1984 that a migration accord be signed with Cuba. The essence of that agreement was that Cuba would accept the repatriation of 2,746 "excludables" and that the United States would renew the processes for permitting the legal immigration of Cubans — up to 20,000 a year, which was the maximum permissible for any single country under the U.S. immigration laws at the time. Around 3,000 former prisoners (those imprisoned for counter-revolutionary crimes) and their relatives would be added to that figure every year; Cuba considered this a moral duty of the United States, since it was the instigator of those individuals' activities.

Even though the U.S. authorities stated that the figure of "up to 20,000" served only to establish a range and not a pledge, the Cubans assumed both in the context of the talks and in the content of the joint communiqué which announced the agreement, that the U.S. government would make the required effort to make maximum use of that figure.[38]

In short, the agreement met the expectations of both governments only in a very limited way. Because of its own laws, the United States was able to send barely half of the original list of 2,476 "excludables" back to Cuba, and the number of those cases continued to increase, because other individuals were included in that category. Moreover, the number of visas granted to Cuban emigrants continued to be much lower than 20,000 a year. In addition, the Cuban government canceled the agreement in May 1985 in response to the initiation of broadcasts by Radio

---

[38] Castro, "Comparecencia ante la televisión," 3.

Martí, a U.S. government station used exclusively for beaming propaganda at Cuba. At that time, also, the Cuban government refused to allow émigrés living in the United States to enter Cuba except for humanitarian reasons. Even though this decision was made more flexible in 1986, the number of such visits that were approved was quite small.

For its part, the U.S. government refused to let people linked to the Cuban government enter the United States, and it interpreted that category extremely widely. The ban on U.S. citizens traveling to Cuba was resurrected using the argument that the blockade prohibited the spending of money that would benefit the Cuban government in any way; regulations were imposed on sending money and on other forms of family assistance; and the U.S. companies which handled such things had to comply with a whole series of unique legal and fiscal prerequisites.

Except for the 1,227 people who emigrated before the agreement was canceled, the migratory flow between the two countries was practically halted until 1988, when in the interest of both governments it was reestablished. In that year, the U.S. government granted 3,472 visas, and, from then up to August 1994, the number of visas granted averaged around 1,000 a year — 6,523 in five and a half years, with the agreement honored completely only with regard to the former prisoners, until the requests in that category were fulfilled.[39]

In view of the minimal number of visas granted, many émigrés left illegally, while others opted for going to a third country from which they requested entry to the United States. This procedure, which would appear to be irregular and time-wasting, was favored because of the existence of the Exodus program in the United States, by means of which the U.S. government gave the Cuban American National Foundation the prerogative to act as surety and insurer for Cuban immigrants living outside Cuba, a power never before granted to a private entity. That program functioned between 1991 and 1993,

---

[39] "These data speak for themselves," *Granma*, Havana, August 25, 1994.

receiving close to $3 million in government assistance. Through it, around 8,000 Cuban immigrants entered the United States, a figure higher than the number of Cubans in Cuba who were authorized to emigrate.[40] Moreover, the U.S. government arbitrarily included the number of Cubans entering from third countries as part of the quota it had agreed on with the Cuban government.

These immigrants entered the United States without the right to receive social welfare. The Foundation's plan guaranteed such assistance by means of private mechanisms, through contributions by their relatives in the United States. The director of refugee assistance in Florida stated that the social security services available to those who immigrated through that program were "atrocious" and even questioned how honestly the funds were handled, criticizing the fact that the contracted insurance company was inexplicably foreign and wasn't subject to the same level of control as its U.S. counterparts. The Foundation exerted pressure on the state government and forced it to retract the statements, to calm the storm that was raised in Florida concerning this matter.[41]

Cuba's policy on emigration

Between 1959 and 1978, Cuba's policy on emigration was characterized by confrontation, both with would-be emigrants before they left and with those who lived abroad.

During that period, the U.S. government organized the Cuban counterrevolution, mainly based on the émigré community, and hundreds of counterrevolutionary groups were formed in the United States and other countries, especially in Central America. The first and best-known of those projects was the 1961 Bay of Pigs invasion, in which around 1,300 émigrés participated, plus an undetermined number of others who, as CIA agents, took part in infiltration and sabotage operations in Cuba.

---

[40] Fonzi, "Mas Canosa," 119.
[41] Fonzi, "Mas Canosa."

When the Bay of Pigs invasion failed, the U.S. government followed it up with Operation Mongoose, a complex plan of subversion in which top U.S. leaders and government institutions were involved. In addition to a wide range of terrorist and paramilitary activities, it also included the imposition of the economic blockade and Cuba's expulsion from the OAS, both carried out in 1962.

From the paramilitary point of view, Operation Mongoose was aimed at promoting social upheaval in Cuba that would justify U.S. military intervention. The émigrés played a key role in implementing it and in the actions which, while organized abroad, involved the infiltration of agents, acts of sabotage, the organization and supplying of bands of rebels, attacks on fishing boats and merchant vessels, and assassination attempts against the main leaders of the revolution. It is estimated that 5,780 counterrevolutionary actions were carried out in the years when Operation Mongoose was in effect. Seven hundred and sixteen of them were acts of sabotage at key targets in Cuba's economy.[42]

The largest CIA station in the world was created in Miami to carry out Operation Mongoose. Hundreds of U.S. officials and thousands of Cuban agents recruited from among the émigrés were on its payroll. In many regards, its operational infrastructure changed the economic, political and social base of southern Florida.

> The arithmetic here is impressive. Even the minimum figures, 300 case officers each running four principal agents who in turn ran 10 regular agents, yield 120,000 regular agents, each of whom might be presumed to have contacts of his own.[43]

The operation was discontinued when the United States and the Soviet Union reached an agreement for ending the 1962 Missile Crisis, but it didn't prevent the U.S. government from

---

[42] Fabián Escalante, *The secret war — CIA covert operations against Cuba 1959-62* (Ocean Press, Melbourne, 1995).

[43] Joan Didion, *Miami*, p. 90.

continuing to plan counterrevolutionary activities against Cuba, based mainly within the émigré community. That agreement, along with the dismantling of the bands of rebels in Cuba and the arrest of the main underground agents, led to a greater concentration of counterrevolutionary activities abroad. In order that their participation in each operation could be "plausibly denied," the U.S. government increased the role of the émigré counterrevolutionary groups and the number of activities carried out from third countries.

This situation remained unchanged until the U.S. involvement in the Vietnam War reached the point where it had to turn the focus away from Cuba. In spite of that, the groups of counterrevolutionary émigrés were quite active against Cuba's coasts throughout the 1960s, and they increased their actions in the 1970s, carrying out terrorist actions against Cuba's personnel and installations in the United States and other countries. One of the most aggressive terrorist networks in the world was created.

Cuba's emigration regulations in the first 20 years of the revolutionary period clearly reflected this state of belligerency. The Cuban regulations stated that those who emigrated could not return, their possessions were confiscated, and those who asked for permission to emigrate were given the worst jobs. Cuban citizens weren't allowed to visit the United States, and the émigrés weren't allowed to visit Cuba. Contact was practically suspended, except for mail and telephone calls, but both of these were limited by the blockade and other obstacles. Other factors that contributed to the gulf, as has already been explained, were the class nature of the first group of émigrés and the fact that they had taken nearly all their relatives with them.

Those regulations were also applied to other Western capitalist countries, which were generally used as bridges for getting to the United States. They weren't applied to the socialist countries or to many other Third World countries with which Cuba maintained close cooperative relations and contacts of various kinds, with plenty of tourism in both directions; academic, cultural and technical exchanges; and internationalist cooperation. Even though the number of émigrés to those countries wasn't large in comparative terms, they were treated differently from those who emigrated to the United States. For example, according to data provided by Cuba's Migration Department, a total of 7,131 Cubans visited other socialist countries as tourists between 1976 and 1979 — data on previous years are not available — and another 3,133 traveled abroad for personal reasons in 1978 and 1979.

Therefore, it may be said that, even though economic and political factors limited the ability of Cuban citizens to travel and settle in certain countries, this wasn't the product of an isolationist policy on Cuba's part. During that same period, Cuba maintained a high level of contact with the rest of the world. In the case of the United States, however, Cuba's emigration policy was quite rigid, and relations with the émigrés were very limited.

As we have already seen, the 1978 dialogue changed this situation, and steps were taken that in the long run have been essentially irreversible, among other reasons because those who emigrated from that year on had different motivations and reflected a different social composition and were therefore viewed differently by Cuban society — which also maintained closer ties with them.

The Mariel events, however, saw a suspension of this process and temporarily restricted relations with those who had emigrated. Starting in 1980, even though the émigrés continued to visit Cuba quite regularly, various formulas were applied to control the number of those visits. Between 1981 and 1985, around 47,000 émigrés visited from the United States. During that period, no one who had emigrated after 1979 was authorized to return on a visit, except for humanitarian reasons. At the same time, the rules governing those who had emigrated prior to 1959 and those living in other countries were liberalized, and their visits to Cuba were facilitated. Between 1980 and 1989, a total of 91,581 Cubans visited the other socialist countries as tourists.[44]

---

[44] Data provided by the Cuban Migration Department.

Starting in 1981, Cuban citizens were authorized to visit the United States. At first, only retired people were allowed to do so — men over 60 and women over 55 — but later the age limit was made more flexible, and now anyone who is over 18 may visit. As a result of this policy, an average of 30,000 Cuban citizens traveled to the United States each year,[45] with (according to figures provided by Cuba's Migration Department) 90 percent of them returning to Cuba, even though they could have used the opportunity to request political asylum in the United States.

From 1987, the number of émigrés authorized to visit Cuba was increased and a category of "humanitarian permission" was also established, for people with relatives who were seriously ill in Cuba. This last step did away with quotas and the migration procedures were simplified for those cases.

With regard to other countries, more authorizations to live abroad were granted. Individuals availing themselves of this policy were able to emigrate while retaining their property in Cuba. In some cases, their jobs were kept open for them, so they could return whenever they wanted. Between 1983 and 1989, a total of 3,339 people were given these authorizations.[46]

In addition to these measures, diverse mechanisms were created to facilitate direct correspondence and the sending of packages and family assistance. Despite 12 years of Republican hostility and an increase in counterrevolutionary activities, relations between Cuba and the Cuban American community were maintained and even strengthening.

Nevertheless, difficulties still remain in Cuba's relations with its émigrés, especially with those who settled in the United States — problems that will be difficult to overcome in the short term. Key to these relations is the counterrevolutionary role which the main political sectors of the community continue to play and their predominantly conservative tendencies — making communication difficult. Along with this is the effect of their integration into U.S. society, which has changed the national identity of most of the émigrés.

---

[45] Castro, "Comparecencia ante la televisión," 3.
[46] Data provided by the Cuban Migration Department.

The problem of citizenship

Neither Cuban nor U.S. law allows dual citizenship. Both require their citizens to renounce their loyalty to any other government, and both state that those who violate this condition and serve the interests of other nations (including native-born citizens) can lose their citizenship.

U.S. law states clearly that to obtain U.S. citizenship one must support the Constitution of the United States; renounce all loyalty and fidelity to any state or foreign sovereignty of which the petitioner was formerly a subject or a citizen; support and defend the Constitution and laws of the United States against all enemies, both external and internal; profess fidelity and loyalty to those laws; and defend the country if requested to do so.[47] Those naturalized in other countries, those who swear loyalty to any other government or who serve in the armed forces of another foreign government, those who renounce their U.S. citizenship and those who commit acts of treason or bear arms against the United States lose their U.S. citizenship.[48]

In the case of Cuba, both the 1902 and 1940 Constitutions support the criterion of exclusive citizenship. This reflects both the need for national reaffirmation, which has been deeply rooted in the Cuban people ever since the Wars of Independence — Cuba was one of the few Latin American countries that was a nation before a country — and the requirements of a political reality which couldn't ignore the U.S. desire for dominance.

The fact that over a million people have emigrated to the United States and more than 60 percent of them have U.S. citizenship, plus the role they have played in the U.S. policy against Cuba since the 1959 revolution, illustrates the importance of this issue. In 1992, as part of the amendments that were made to the Cuban Constitution, the section on citizenship was changed, setting only the general principles and making the law

---

[47] Judiciary Committee of the U.S. House of Representatives. *Ley de Inmigración y Nacionalidad con enmiendas y notas sobre leyes relacionadas* [Immigration and Citizenship Act with amendments and notes on related laws], 216. Spanish version.
[48] Immigration Act, 234.

responsible for determining specific points. At the time of writing, the Cuban National Assembly was discussing a draft Citizenship Law, which would simplify the understanding and the mechanisms related to this matter but did not make any basic conceptual changes. It reaffirmed that those who acquired another citizenship would lose their Cuban citizenship, and that those who served another nation without the permission of the Cuban government, those who committed acts against the security of the Cuban government and those who swore loyalty to another government would be deprived of their citizenship.[49]

The rejection of dual citizenship has remained unchanged throughout Cuba's national history, and the revolution reaffirmed it. However, for several reasons, including those of national security and practicality — and also to ensure that a large number of émigrés would not be left stranded, without any citizenship — this constitutional precept hasn't been strictly applied. To the contrary, émigrés who have adopted other citizenship but who want to travel to Cuba must have up-to-date Cuban passports — a situation which has created an obviously contradictory legal precedent.

This situation also has political consequences, for the rights and duties of émigrés and their descendants with regard to the Cuban nation haven't been clarified adequately. Moreover, this ambiguity has made it possible for émigré organizations to declare themselves Cuban or U.S. at will, whichever most suits them at the time, in violation of the laws of both countries.

This lack of clarity also makes it easier for other countries, either out of ignorance or in response to U.S. pressures, to demand that Cuba grant political rights to its émigrés, most of whom are in the United States and, in both existential and legal terms, have ceased to be Cuban citizens.

In its essential aspects, Cuba's position of limiting the political rights of its émigrés follows the common practice of governments with their émigrés and doesn't necessarily imply a

---

[49] Juridical Affairs Commission of the Cuban National Assembly of People's Power. *Anteproyecto de Ley de Ciudadanía* [Draft of the Citizenship Law], version 4, 7-8.

deterioration of relations. The Cuban government's sponsorship of the Nation and Emigration conference in April 1994 was an important step in searching for a way to confront this problem.

The Nation and Emigration conference

In October 1993, the Cuban government announced its intention of holding a new meeting with representatives of the Cuban community abroad, to discuss the problems that affected their links with the Cuban nation. Many, including the Cuban government itself, considered this conference to be a continuation of the 1978 dialogue, even though the context in which this meeting was to be held was a far cry from that of the earlier dialogue.

The conditions that facilitated the 1978 dialogue included an improvement in relations with the United States, so one of its main purposes was to ease tensions with the Cuban community in the United States. Such was not the case with the Clinton administration, which had adopted the Torricelli Law as the basis of its policy on Cuba and has maintained a firm alliance with the Cuban American extreme right.

Further, the 1978 dialogue had been held at a time when the counterrevolution was in moral bankruptcy. Therefore, one of the main decisions reached was that the Cuban government would release nearly all the counterrevolutionaries who were still serving time. But from 1980, U.S. policy gave counterrevolutionary activities a tremendous boost, activities which were also promoted by the rightwing euphoria that accompanied the collapse of the socialist camp and the dismemberment of the Soviet Union.

In 1978, the Cuban economy was in a relatively good period, but the 1994 Nation and Emigration conference was held during the worst economic crisis faced by Cuban society. In fact, the crisis determined the characteristics of the meeting, since the meeting couldn't be isolated from the country's efforts to adapt to the conditions imposed by the international situation.

The organizers of the conference hoped that it would help to solve problems of links with the émigrés and promote the normalization of Cuba's relations with them.[50] It was hoped that this would lead to a situation similar to those of other countries, whose émigrés contributed to the national economies of their country of origin.

Several measures were taken: a department was created in the Ministry of Foreign Affairs to handle this problem; the prerequisite that émigrés would have to wait at least five years after leaving Cuba before visiting it again was eliminated; a number of young émigrés were accepted as students in Cuba's universities; some of the prerequisites for traveling to Cuba were made more flexible; the problem of citizenship was reviewed; and the Cuban government announced its willingness to continue these meetings in the future.[51]

Some of the top Cuban leaders gave the émigré representatives an explanation of the economic situation, the system of popular participation in government and national culture, and those attending the meeting were invited to an official reception which President Fidel Castro attended.

Parallel with the conference, a session of the Commission of Juridical Affairs of the National Assembly was held to analyze problems related to citizenship and some of the participants in the conference were invited to address the session. Even though it wasn't given much attention by the national and foreign press, this constituted an important indication of the conditions in which the Cuban government thought those relations could develop, even at the political level, and a precedent was set for future relations.[52]

New measures followed a few months later. The age at which people could be authorized to make visits abroad was lowered to 18; the time authorized for visits abroad for personal reasons was lengthened from 6 to 11 months; repatriation was allowed under certain conditions; authorizations were broadened

---

[50] Roberto Robaina, *Discurso de apertura en la conferencia la Nación y la Emigración* [Opening address in the Nation and Emigration conference].
[51] *Contrapunto*, June 1994, 12.
[52] *Contrapunto*, 25.

for living abroad and those living abroad with such authorizations no longer had to request permission to visit Cuba.[53]

This policy was abruptly interrupted, however, when as a result of the migration crisis of August 1994 the Clinton administration took measures that made it practically impossible for émigrés to maintain relations with their country of origin — measures which no other U.S. administration had taken, even at times of greatest tension.

---

[53] "Interview with José Cabañas," *Granma*, Havana, August 25, 1994, 2.

CHAPTER 3

Crisis and emigration

In 1959, around 80 percent of Cuba's imports came from and 60 percent of its exports went to the U.S. market. This trade was one of the most concentrated in the world.[54] U.S. investments in Cuba amounted to between $700 million and $1 billion and controlled the most profitable sectors of Cuban industry and services. In the case of the sugar industry, the key to the Cuban economy, U.S. consortia owned 36 sugar mills, which concentrated 42 percent of the production and controlled 1,474,000 hectares of land, much of which was kept idle as a sugarcane reserve.[55]

The Cuban economy's practically total subordination to the U.S. market included technology, a large part of the infrastructure and professional training, credits, investments and the focus of development. In those circumstances, the introduction of the U.S. blockade forced Cuba to restructure its economic base, foreign trade and development strategy, leading to the decision to join the other socialist countries in the Council for Mutual Economic Assistance.

---

[54] Ramón Armas, Francisco López Segrera, and Germán Sánchez, *Los partidos políticos en Cuba neocolonial 1899-1952* [Political parties in neocolonial Cuba, 1899-1959], 168-170.
[55] Oscar Pino Santos, *El Asalto a Cuba por la oligarquía financiera yanki* [The attack on Cuba by the U.S. financial oligarchy], 197-211.

Economic blockade and Cuba joins the socialist camp

The economic blockade of Cuba was conceived in the ideological framework of the Monroe Doctrine. Therefore, it was always aimed at third countries as the United States felt that it had the right to demand that its allies and trading partners respect and adopt the blockade.

Starting in 1959, the Eisenhower administration took measures cutting back on trade with Cuba, and these culminated in October 1960 with a ban on exporting to Cuba any U.S. product other than food or medicines. On February 3, 1962, as part of a covert action program against Cuba, codenamed Operation Mongoose, President Kennedy issued a decree broadening that prohibition to all imports from Cuba. Two years later President Johnson added food and medicines to the list of proscribed articles.[56]

Those decisions deprived the Cuban economy of what had been its main market for nearly 200 years — a market that was also the biggest in the world. But the blockade went further: it also froze Cuba's accounts in U.S. banks; forbade U.S. citizens to trade with Cuban firms in other countries, spend money in Cuba or send money to anyone in Cuba; closed the U.S. market to foreign products from any country that contained Cuban components; forbade the foreign subsidiaries of U.S. companies to trade with Cuba; refused to allow international financial agencies to grant credits to Cuba; and even forbade other countries to use dollars in their transactions with Cuba.

The blockade has been particularly rigid with regard to shipping. Several mechanisms have been used to punish ships carrying trade to Cuba or which visit Cuban ports either before or after arriving in U.S. territory. Terrorist organizations of Cuban émigrés, usually linked to the CIA, have also operated against Cuban shipping, even resorting to sinking and hijacking ships.

The blockade has cost Cuba an estimated $41 billion. It reduced Cuba's purchasing power by 40 percent in 1993 alone,

---

[56] Nicanor León Cotayo, *Sitiada la esperanza* [Hope besieged], 50.

causing a considerable increase in freight, interest and insurance rates and in the prices paid by Cuba.[57]

The socialist market gave Cuba preferential prices, credits and an integrated framework which enabled it to refocus its development with relative security. As a result of the restrictions which the blockade imposed and the advantages of the socialist market, which handled 85 percent of Cuba's exports and imports in 1989, the socialist bloc was Cuba's main source of technology and scientific and professional exchanges.[58]

The collapse of the socialist camp — especially the dismembering of the Soviet Union in 1991 — once again radically changed the bases of Cuba's economy, but this time there were no other options outside the U.S. sphere of influence, as there had been in the 1960s.

The magnitude and speed of this impact submerged the country into the most drastic crisis of its history. By 1993, Cuba's purchasing power had dropped from $8.2 billion to less than $2 billion — that is, it could purchase only 23 percent as much in 1993 as in 1989.[59] In addition, it had no credit, no preferential prices, and even no guarantee that if it had the cash on hand it could purchase the products it needed, since the blockade and the internal disorder in the former socialist countries made this doubtful.

In short, U.S. specialists estimate that Cuba's GNP dropped by 50 percent in three years, 600 investment projects (including a nuclear power project that was to have provided a third of the electricity the country needed) were paralyzed and the value of the Cuban peso on the black market dropped from 8 to 100 to the dollar.[60]

This situation totally disorganized Cuba's economic system, the mechanisms of state planning became impracticable, the

---

[57] Carlos Lage, *Intervención en la conferencia La Nación y la Emigración* [Address in the Nation and Emigration conference], 9.

[58] Lage, 1.

[59] Lage, 5.

[60] Carmelo Mesa Lago, "Will Cuba's economic reform work?," *Miami Herald*, January 2, 1994, 1-A.

foreign market reduced its options, the economy became decentralized, the premises for its functioning were radically changed, and everything became much more expensive; industries had to be shut down, quality standards revised and production rechanneled. Unemployment and underemployment rose to levels unprecedented in the revolutionary period, so certain branches of welfare had to be increased and investments in other important sectors such as public health and education had to be reduced. Recreational and cultural options were seriously cut back; Cubans' daily lives became filled with overwhelming problems related to shortages of transportation, electricity and access to other services; and crime began to rise with the deterioration in the work ethic and social consciousness (as a result of the devaluation of wages).

In those conditions, U.S. policy was aimed at speeding the collapse of the Cuban revolution, which many officials in Washington thought was now inevitable. The blockade was tightened in the hope that it would finally succeed and strangle Cuba. This strategy received bipartisan support and became official policy with the approval of the Cuban Democracy Act, commonly known as the Torricelli Act (named after the Democratic representative who sponsored it), in 1992.

The Torricelli Act
Lacking the excuse of Soviet containment, the Torricelli Act focused exclusively on demands related to the Cuban domestic situation and expressly acknowledged that its purpose was to promote a change in Cuba's political system. In its Statement of Policy, the Act declares that the U.S. government's policy on Cuba should be:

> to seek a peaceful solution to democracy and a resumption of economic growth in Cuba through the careful application of sanctions directed at the Castro government [and] to make clear to other countries that, in determining its relations with them, the United States

will take into account their willingness to cooperate in such policy. . . .[61]

It is interesting to note that the Torricelli Act once again resorts to the argument that Cubans who leave their country do so for political reasons:

> The Cuban people have demonstrated their yearning for freedom and their increasing opposition to the Castro government by risking their lives in organizing independent, democratic activities on the island and by undertaking hazardous flights for freedom to the United States and other countries. . . .[62]

The law demands that sanctions be applied against countries that don't collaborate with that strategy and, even though it approves certain forms of nongovernmental humanitarian assistance and the extension of communications, considering them a means of ideological influence, it strengthens the mechanisms of the economic blockade, even prohibiting the foreign subsidiaries of U.S. companies from trading with Cuba.[63]

The extraterritoriality of the Torricelli Act led to protests by the international community and contributed to the UN General Assembly passing condemnations of the economic blockade against Cuba by wide margins in 1992, 1993, 1994 and again in 1995. This, however, didn't prevent the Bush and Clinton administrations from beefing up the blockade, and, according to Torricelli himself, business between the foreign subsidiaries of U.S. companies and Cuba dropped from $718 million in 1991 to $1.6 million in 1993.[64]

Even though none of the main currents in U.S. foreign policy favored that course of action, because of the conflicts it could generate with other countries, the advocates of that policy

---

[61] "Cuban Democracy Act of 1992," *Congressional Record*, 1992, p. 271.
[62] "Cuban Democracy Act," 270.
[63] "Cuban Democracy Act," 270-77.
[64] Robert Torricelli, "Letter to *The Miami Herald*," January 5, 1994.

promoted by the sectors of the Cuban American ultraright acted in hope that Cuba's economic strangulation would cause social chaos that would justify U.S. intervention. To achieve their goal, they took advantage of the 1992 election in the United States and, by means of pressures and deals, managed to compromise both candidates and obtain the nearly unanimous support of Congress. Even institutions such as the CIA warned of the consequences that chaos caused in Cuban society might have for the United States.[65]

Cuba has managed to withstand those pressures and has taken steps to adapt its economy to the demands of the present international situation without resorting to neoliberal "shock therapy." It has not, however, been able to avoid a substantial drop in the people's standard of living, and this has caused a growing number of Cubans to pin their hopes on emigration. Since they have no viable legal alternatives and U.S. propaganda promotes illegal departures, many of those individuals decided to emigrate from Cuba illegally.

Illegal emigrants

Cuban laws require that each émigré have a passport, a visa from another country and authorization to emigrate. Illegal emigration is that which doesn't fulfill these prerequisites. The United States also considers every immigrant who lacks a visa to be there illegally. Even so, since U.S. immigration laws had granted asylum to every Cuban who reached U.S. territory in the past, illegal émigrés availed themselves of several variants, such as temporary visas to the United States and the hijacking of planes and ships. Cuban officials who abandoned their missions abroad, and cultural and sports figures who asked for permission to go to the United States from other countries have always been accepted without restrictions. Other would-be émigrés have occasionally forced their way into embassies in Cuba. However, the most common practice has been for émigrés to take to the sea in any kind of vessel, trusting that once outside Cuba's territorial

---

[65] Carla Ann Robbins, "CIA tells Clinton he could face a crisis in Cuba if serious instability develops," *Wall Street Journal*, November 2, 1993, 1.

waters someone would pick them up and take them to the United States.

A whole system was in operation to facilitate those illegal departures. First of all, the U.S. Coast Guard units that patrolled the area regularly had instructions to pick up and take those Cubans to the United States. Sometimes, paradoxically, Haitian émigrés trying to reach the United States illegally would pick up shipwrecked Cubans and, when intercepted by U.S. Coast Guards, would be sent back to Haiti by force, while the Cubans were given preferential treatment and automatically accepted. Any ship could pick up the illegal Cuban émigrés and inform the U.S. Coast Guard, which would immediately go to help them, and a private organization called "Hermanos del Rescate" was created which engaged in air patrols in the area to detect rafters on the high seas and report their positions to the U.S. authorities. It is clear that the chance of rescue from such an adventure was relatively high, which was an incentive for such departures.

Thus, a rather amazing situation in international relations (though it was also the case in U.S. relations with the former socialist countries) was created in which Cuba had to protect its borders, trying to prevent illegal emigration, while the United States, the country receiving those illegal emigrants, welcomed them and gave them preferential treatment, contradicting its own immigration system. Therefore, illegal emigration has had its ups and downs, depending on many factors, including the domestic situation in Cuba, the pressures for family reunification and the facilities the United States has provided for those trying to emigrate legally from Cuba.

There are no exact figures on the number of Cubans who used that means for emigrating to the United States in the first few years after 1959 (U.S. statistics don't consider any Cubans who reached the United States after the revolution to be illegal immigrants[66]), but it would be fair to assume that a large number

---

[66] Antonio Aja Díaz, "La emigración ilegal hacia Estados Unidos" [Illegal emigration to the United States], *Areíto*, March 1994, 5.

of the over 26,000 Cubans[67] who emigrated in 1959 did so without the official authorization of the U.S. government.

Between the time the regular flights between Cuba and the United States were suspended in 1962 and the signing of the first migration agreements in 1965, an estimated 29,000 people — 30 percent of all the emigrants in that period — emigrated illegally.[68] The establishment of a normal migratory channel, together with the possibility the would-be emigrants had for meeting U.S. legal requirements, considerably reduced the illegal flow, so only around 20,500 people left Cuba illegally in the next eight years.[69] In the 1973-79 period, even though the air bridge had been canceled, there was a reduction in emigration in all its forms.

In view of the contradictory way in which U.S. immigration laws were applied, it is impossible to determine with any certainty whether the United States considers those who left Cuba through Mariel as legal or illegal immigrants, although, from Cuba's point of view, they emigrated legally, with their documents in order.

Unlike the situation in 1965, the 1984 migration agreement concerned a group of would-be émigrés who did not meet U.S. requirements. Since the priorities set by U.S. law were practically the same, the difference lay in the composition of those who wanted to emigrate and in the degree of family ties they had in the United States. The inflexible application of those parameters meant that, between 1985 and 1990, only 7,428 people were able to emigrate legally — out of the possible 100,000 established by the agreements.[70] Even so, there wasn't an increase in illegal departures; to the contrary, these dropped to the lowest numbers since the revolution: only 1,000 in the five-year period.[71] That element should be noted, because it reflected a relatively high degree of social stability in Cuba until the economic crisis

---

[67] Masud-Piloto, *With open arms*, 3.
[68] Arce, *La emigración*, 3.
[69] Arce, *La emigración*, 6.
[70] Castro, "Comparecencia ante la televisión," 3.
[71] Aja Díaz, *La emigración ilegal*, 8.

developed in 1991, and the numbers of people leaving the country illegally rocketed again.

Between 1991 and July 1994, the United States welcomed 12,808 illegal Cuban émigrés, while it approved only 3,794 requests for legal entry.[72] This contradiction is the basis for Cuba's claim that the U.S. immigration policy toward Cuba hasn't been applied in good faith. One of the most graphic descriptions of this situation was given by U.S. diplomat Jay Taylor, who was head of the U.S. Interests Section in Cuba between 1987 and 1990:

> Of all the ironies in American foreign policy today, our course on Cuba is the most paradoxical. Sharply deteriorating economic conditions have caused a surge in the number of Cubans fleeing illegally to the United States. We do everything we can unilaterally to worsen the economy and thus increase the flow. We also directly encourage the exodus by granting Cubans who arrive illegally or who are headed this way on the high seas resident status and resettlement assistance. At the same time, we have unfilled immigration and political refugee quotas for Cubans who wish to immigrate to the United States [. . .] when Castro tries to stop unhappy Cubans from fleeing his benighted land, we accuse him of human rights abuse. But when he threatens to open the floodgates if we continue to welcome unlimited numbers of undocumented Cubans, including those who have committed violent acts in the course of their departure, we warn unspecified but ominous consequences.[73]

In addition, radio stations, including those spreading U.S. government policy, have encouraged illegal departures of Cubans in various ways through 1,700 hours of programming a week,

---

[72] Castro, "Comparecencia ante la televisión," 1.
[73] Jay Taylor, "Playing into Castro's hands," *The Guardian*, London, August 9, 1994.

over dozens of medium-wave and short-wave frequencies.[74] But perhaps what has been exploited most extensively to directly and indirectly stimulate Cubans' emigration, especially by young people, those most likely to go the illegal sea route, has been the promotion of Miami as a place where any enterprising individual can get whatever he or she wants.

According to studies made recently by a multidisciplinary group from the University of Havana, using a sample of almost 100 would-be illegal émigrés from Havana, "At the beginning of the 1970s, the difference in the Cuban migratory pattern grew deeper, becoming progressively more related to certain sectors of the present sociodemographic structure of Cuba." Moreover, "these aren't individuals who were left behind by other migratory waves," since they decided to emigrate when the crisis began, seeking a means to achieve their personal aspirations, which they believed could not be attained in Cuba. Most of those in the sample studied were workers, followed by technicians, professionals and the self-employed, in line with the social structure of Havana. The proportion of young, white men was higher than in earlier groups of émigrés.[75]

On the basis of those indicators, it can be said that the new émigrés are people prepared to take up the challenge of migration and, therefore, seek to widen their options in a more developed society, even though as the study shows most of them didn't consider the American way of life an ideal social model, but preferred Cuban society before the crisis.

This situation therefore reflects a different historical moment, and thus the motivations that impelled the group to emigrate and their social composition are essentially different.

Even though the "Mariel syndrome" has been a permanent concern of the U.S. authorities in the last decade, U.S. policy incited this emigration, trusting that the restrictions Cuba placed on illegal departures would keep the volume of émigrés within levels that could be absorbed economically and politically with-

---

[74] "Information from the government of Cuba to national and international public opinion," *Granma*, September 14, 1994, 1.
[75] Aja Díaz, *La emigración ilegal*, 8.

out too much trouble. In fact, the Cuban government kept 37,801 people from leaving the country illegally between January 1990 and July 1994.[76]

---

[76] Castro, "Comparecencia ante la televisión," 1.

CHAPTER 4

The 1994 migration accord

On July 13, 1994, a group of people hijacked a Cuban tugboat in order to take it to the United States, despite the fact that the boat was over 100 years old and would never survive on the high seas. When three other tugboats belonging to the same enterprise tried to stop it, there was an accident that took the lives of 32 of the 63 occupants of the boat. U.S. Secretary of State Warren Christopher stated in the U.S. Congress that the incident was a reminder of the "brutal" nature of the Cuban regime and of the need for an alternative government that would return the country to the "democratic days" prior to the revolution.[77]

On July 26, two more vessels were hijacked — this time, ferries designed for transporting passengers within the Bay of Havana. To avoid more accidents, those vessels were escorted by Cuban Coast Guard vessels, but despite this a Cuban police officer who happened to be among the passengers was killed. One of the vessels was assisted by U.S. Coast Guard ships, and the hijackers were taken to the United States, where they were immediately given political asylum. The hijackers of the other vessel turned themselves over to Cuban authorities when their fuel ran out while still in Cuban waters.

---

[77] Warren Christopher, statement to the Foreign Affairs Committee of the U.S. House of Representatives, July 28, 1994.

Inspired by the climate generated by these events, groups of anti-government protestors clashed with government supporters in some streets in Havana on August 5. The police intervened, and peace was quickly reestablished. No one was killed and there were few injuries. The U.S. press portrayed the episode as the first rebellion against the Cuban system, and the counter-revolutionary groups abroad described it as the beginning of a popular revolt against the government.

That same night, President Fidel Castro appeared on Cuban television and warned that the United States should stop trying to promote illegal emigration, saying that the Cuban government wouldn't be able to prevent a mass exodus. The reply from White House chief Leon Panetta was that Castro couldn't dictate the migration policy of the United States and that the U.S. government wouldn't allow another Mariel.[78]

On August 8, a Cuban Navy passenger transport ship was hijacked, the hijackers killing one of the officers on board during the action. Even though the Cuban government informed the United States of what had happened and even identified the criminal, the hijackers were welcomed as usual. Later on, the accused was arrested, but he was acquitted by a Miami court for "lack of proof."

On August 9 and 11, the *Washington Post* and *New York Times* carried editorials recommending a review of U.S. policy on Cuba, including the lifting of the blockade. On August 11, in a new appearance on television, Fidel Castro expressed Cuba's willingness to negotiate on the migration problem and on other matters, particularly the economic blockade — which, from the Cuban point of view, was the main cause of the crisis.[79] However, the Secretary of State Warren Christopher responded saying that the United States would not change its Cuba policy and would continue giving preferential treatment to illegal

---

[78] Leon Panetta, statements to the press, August 8, 1994.
[79] Castro, "Comparecencia ante la televisión," 2.

Cuban immigrants — a position which Attorney General Janet Reno ratified.[80]

On August 12, the Cuban government decided to remove restrictions on illegal departures (later on, it stated that minors could not go) and also allowed ships from other countries to come and pick up would-be Cuban emigrants. Three days later, around 700 people seized an oil tanker and tried to take it to the United States. The Cuban authorities warned that it would be dangerous to use that ship for carrying people and persuaded those who had seized it to leave peacefully.

On August 19, the Clinton administration made an about-face in its Cuban migration policy, announcing that the rafters would not be admitted into the United States. They were to be treated like the Haitians and interned in a "safe haven," most of them at the Guantánamo Naval Base. No longer would Cuban émigrés receive the benefits of the Cuban Adjustment Act of 1966, and they wouldn't even be considered for refugee status, even though U.S. immigration laws state that all who ask for asylum must be so considered.

Along with that decision, the U.S. government banned travel to Cuba by Cuban émigrés; closed its doors to Cubans living in Cuba; halted the sending of money and packages — except certain medicines — to Cuba; prohibited travel to Cuba by academics, journalists and other U.S. professionals (unless they obtained specific authorization from the government); and took other measures to "tighten the embargo against Cuba and thereby limit the ability of the Cuban government to accumulate foreign exchange." Violators would be liable to penalties of up to 10 years in prison and fines of from $250,000 to $1 million.[81] It also announced that the United States would take the subject of Cuba to the United Nations Security Council and that it would

---

[80] Warren Christopher, "Declaraciones a la prensa el 13 de agosto de 1994" [Statements to the press, August 13, 1994], EFE, August 13, 1994.

[81] Office of Foreign Assets Control, Department of the Treasury. *New regulations on Cuba affecting mailing of gift packages, travel and remittances of funds to Cuba.*

extend and intensify its radio and television broadcasts beamed at Cuban territory.

The U.S. President made his position perfectly clear, stating that his country had done more than any other to put an end to Castro's government, even though it had sometimes been alone in that policy, and that it would continue acting in that way with all reasonable means at its disposal.[82]

President Fidel Castro summarized the situation:

> Unquestionably, for the first time, there is an attempt to discourage — or to take some measures that will discourage — illegal departures, but [Clinton's] decision to send them to the Guantánamo Naval Base is absurd, from our point of view, and it only complicates the problem. . . . I said that the blockade was a basic, compelling element, and they responded by tightening it. I said that the subversive broadcasts constantly incited people to leave illegally, and they responded by increasing their broadcasts. . . . In this case, with a single stroke, the U.S. government has destroyed the work of years aimed at creating a climate of harmony and family unification for the Cubans who are in Cuba and those who are abroad.[83]

What lay behind the U.S. decisions

Factors of a domestic nature always influence the foreign policy decisions of any country, but the immigration issue has been particularly sensitive in the United States because of its impact on the economy, its ideological context, its weight in international relations and its consequences on U.S. national security.

The prospect of a massive, uncontrolled wave of Cuban immigrants may have had negative implications for the Democratic administration, especially in the State of Florida where the Governor was running for reelection and his victory

---

[82] Pablo Alfonso, "Clinton pasa a la ofensiva" [Clinton takes the offensive], *El Nuevo Herald*, August 20, 1994, 1.
[83] Castro, "Comparecencia ante la televisión," 3.

was considered essential for Clinton's own options in 1996. The decision to concentrate the émigrés at the Guantánamo Naval Base sought to place the problem outside U.S. territory, so as to limit its political impact and avoid the obligations implicit in their arrival in the United States.

A poll taken by Florida International University among residents in Dade County showed that 66 percent supported the measures,[84] even though 59 percent of the sample were of Cuban origin and, of whom, only 24 percent supported this policy.[85] It may be assumed that areas with lower concentrations of Cubans would have shown greater support, so the government achieved what it had set out to do, facilitating the reelection of Governor Lawton Chiles.

The Cuban American population's opposition to the new policy was understandable, not only because of the emotional ties involved — especially for the relatives of those affected — but also because this decision was a blow against the preferential treatment which they had been granted historically. Those who supported the measure were those in a better social position, whose interests went beyond the framework of the enclave. This may have been why the Cuban American city manager stated that, in spite of the survey's results, the main groups in the Cuban American community supported this policy, because of the implication that the massive arrival of those immigrants would have for the region.[86]

To weaken the opposition of Cuban American voters, Clinton decided to meet with a delegation from Miami and adopt the proposals made by the CANF president for tightening the blockade. By so doing, he also tried to neutralize criticism by Republican congressmen of Cuban origin who were calling for a tougher stand on Cuba.

---

[84] Maydel Santana, "Encuesta: Cubano-americanos rechazan envíos a Guantánamo" [Poll: Cuban Americans oppose sending émigrés to Guantánamo], *El Nuevo Herald*, August 21, 1994, 1.

[85] Santana, "Encuesta."

[86] Francisco García Agüero, "Sector privado teme las consecuencias del éxodo" [Private sector fears the consequences of the exodus], *El Nuevo Herald*, September 2, 1994, 1.

Clinton's links with the CANF dated from the 1992 electoral campaign, when in exchange for his support for the Torricelli Act the organization put around $350,000 into his war chest, causing dissent in the leadership of the Foundation, since most of them were Republicans.[87] The Foundation's relations with many conservative sectors in the United States were also damaged, as they felt betrayed.

The 1994 measures taken to limit the relations between the émigrés and their relatives in Cuba polarized the Cuban American community, driving a wedge between the more liberal elements and those with closer emotional ties with the Cuban people, on the one hand, and the conservative sectors, whose top priority was the overthrow of the Cuban government, on the other. This latter group has consistently supported the Republican Party, no matter what the Cuban American National Foundation's attitude has been. At least, that's what happened in 1992, when Clinton won Dade County in spite of opposition by most of the Cuban American voters, and in 1994, when Lawton Chiles, though winning the election, lost the Cuban American vote by a wide margin. Thus, paradoxically, with those decisions, the Democrats may be strengthening their opponents to the detriment of those sectors that, though a minority, are the only ones in the Cuban American community who have traditionally supported them.

The path toward the agreement
In any case, the weight of the Cuban American National Foundation, while apparently overestimated by the Clinton administration at first, has declined as the discussion surrounding the problem of the Cuban rafters went beyond the local scene and took on a national dimension. There is a well-defined consensus in favor of a review of U.S. policy on Cuba that will make it possible to solve the migration problem, avoid a crisis and adapt U.S. strategy to the current international climate.

---

[87] Fonzi, "Mas Canosa," 88.

Such influential papers as the *Washington Post, New York Times* and *Wall Street Journal* have come out editorially in favor of a review of U.S. policy on Cuba. Influential Congressmen from both parties — Thomas Foley, former Majority Leader in the House of Representatives; Lee Hamilton, former Chairman of the Foreign Affairs Committee of the House of Representatives[88]; Senators Christopher Dodd (D), Alan Simpson (R) and Richard Lugar (R); and Representatives Charles Rangel (D) and José Serrano (D) — have also called for such a review, as have many of the key U.S. political experts, especially Peter Harkim, Director of Inter-American Dialogue, a group whose members include some of the main foreign policy officials of the present administration. This position is even supported by such an unlikely ally as William Buckley, one of the kingpins in the New Right, who said in this regard, "Our negotiators need to bear in mind that to end the blockade now is not retroactively to discredit it. It is to acknowledge fresh perspectives."[89]

Congressmen from Florida headed by Cuban American Representatives Ileana Ross (R) and Lincoln Díaz-Balart (R) and other political figures such as Robert Torricelli uphold the present policy and even favor increased economic pressures, the application of a naval blockade and armed intervention. Most are publicly involved with the Cuban American extreme right and are quite an isolated group.

This situation made it easier for the Clinton administration to change the focus of its policy, accept many of the principles on which the Cuban position is based and participate in the negotiations that led to the most recent migration accord.

The accord was signed on September 9, 1994. It set forth the interest of both governments to prevent dangerous departures from Cuba, the discontinuation of the U.S. policy of automatically admitting all illegal immigrants of Cuban origin and

---

[88] When the Democrats lost their majority in both houses of Congress in the 1994 election, they also lost the posts of Majority Leader and Committee chairmen.

[89] William Buckley, "It's a matter of pride," *The Miami Herald*, September 4, 1994.

the U.S. government's commitment to punish the use of force and hijackings of planes and ships for purposes of emigration. An understanding was also reached for normalizing the legal migratory flow, the U.S. government pledging that it would grant a minimum of 20,000 visas a year and offer facilities to potential Cuban émigrés. For its part, the Cuban government pledged to use essentially persuasive methods to control the illegal emigration from its coasts to the United States.[90]

This agreement was the first of the migration agreements signed by the two countries that was specifically aimed at controlling the illegal emigration — reflecting quite a radical change in the policy that the United States has historically applied to Cuba.

However, the fact that the United States agreed to discuss only this matter, artificially isolating it from other problems affecting the relations between the two countries, and the multiple approaches it used to solve the crisis, striving to please too wide a range of sectors in the U.S. political system, imply the transitory nature of some of the measures and could generate new contradictions in the U.S policy on Cuba.

The retention of around 30,000 Cubans in virtual concentration camps outside U.S. territory raised a legal, political and humanitarian dilemma which the U.S. government had to solve sooner or later. The presence of around 8,000 of those individuals on U.S. military bases in Panama has already had explosive consequences that forced the United States to send them back to the Guantánamo Naval Base. But that raises an even more sensitive issue, because that territory itself is being used against the will of the Cuban government. Furthermore, it is a very dangerous area, with a high level of military concentration, and has been a permanent source of tension. Serious incidents have occurred when hundreds of émigrés sought to flee from the base, crossing the mine fields that lie on both sides of the base's perimeter, endangering both their own lives and those of Cuban soldiers who have gone to their assistance.

---

[90] "Conversaciones Cuba-EE.UU.: Comunicado conjunto" [Cuban-U.S. talks: Joint communiqué], *Granma*, September 10, 1994, 6.

The agreements foresee those people's voluntary return to Cuba. Once in Cuban territory, they may request legal admittance to the United States. Some hundreds have taken up that option, but most preferred to remain on the base, trusting that at some time they would be sent directly to the United States. It was obvious that recognizing that this was an exceptional situation, so as not to spur more illegal departures, the two governments had to search for a solution to that problem.

The ban on travel and other forms of communication between the Cuban American community in the United States and their relatives in Cuba probably won't last long. The Cuban Americans are the only U.S. citizens and residents who may neither travel to their country of origin nor send economic assistance to their relatives. Thus, the Cuban American community is discriminated against in this regard. However, the implicit contradiction between these provisions and the signing of an agreement to normalize the migratory relations between the two countries is even more important. The apparently inevitable reversal of those decisions could be a telling blow for the influence that the Cuban American ultraright has had so far on U.S. policy toward Cuba and for its relations with the Democratic administration.

The 1994 agreements clearly contributed to a different climate between the two nations, as Ricardo Alarcón, who headed the Cuban negotiators, noted when he said, "It is as if we were to tear off an aspect of that hostile and illegal policy and place it on an adequate plane."[91] That is, the agreements were considered a starting point in the sense of an improvement in the relations between the two countries. It wasn't much of an improvement, but things were moving in a direction contrary to that of recent years.

The U.S. political pendulum, however, could easily swing the other way. The results of the 1994 election showed that the

---

[91] José de la Osa, "Califica Alarcón de importancia apreciable acuerdo entre Cuba y EE.UU" [Alarcón describes agreement between Cuba and the U.S. as quite important], *Granma*, September 10, 1994, 6.

Republican extreme right had considerable clout. The migration problem has become the focal point of the conservative campaign, and the approval of decisions such as Proposition 187 in a California referendum announced a flaring up of xenophobia, particularly directed against Hispanics.[92]

Even though fear of an increase in uncontrolled illegal immigration has served as the basis for the consensus reached with Cuba, the anti-immigrant climate promoted by the U.S. ultraright, the weakness demonstrated by the present administration and the interest the Cuban American extreme right has in provoking an escalation in the conflict between the two countries, make it impossible to guarantee that the modus vivendi achieved with the agreements will be irreversible.

The figure of at least 20,000 Cuban immigrants a year is quite appropriate, both quantitatively and qualitatively, compared to the legal models now in effect in the United States. Those individuals would enter the country, under an extraordinary prerogative of the Secretary of Justice; thus, in practice, the quota regime is being violated. This procedure isn't new for the case of the Cubans; it was used quite frequently up to 1962, but this is hardly the same political period, and the private conservative institutions concerned with immigration have already presented legal appeals against that measure.

The Republican victory may have other consequences in the specific case of Cuba, because extraordinarily aggressive positions have clearly been revitalized — as in the case of Senator Jesse Helms, Chairman of the Foreign Relations Committee, who as soon as the result of the election was made known declared that he would work to overthrow the Cuban regime and would even support a military invasion of Cuba.[93]

To promote that policy, Senator Helms and Congressman Burton sponsored a bill on Cuban "democratic freedom." Even though the process of discussion and approval of that bill hasn't

---

[92] There is even talk of limiting the rights of legal immigrants who are not U.S. citizens. See Evan Thomas, "Goodbye welfare state," *Time*, November 24, 1994, 39.

[93] Howard Fineman, "Revenge of the Right," *Time*, November 24, 1994, 39.

been completed at the time this book is going to press, its original version is worth studying, both for an understanding of the philosophy that inspires the ultra-conservative sectors of U.S. policy-makers and as an example of the restorational aims of the Cuban American extreme right.

An analysis of that thinking, how it conflicts with the international order and the fact that it is not feasible as an alternative for Cuba's socioeconomic and political development are beyond the scope of this book. Suffice it to point out that the bill calls for tightening the blockade and extending its extraterritorial scope to levels unprecedented in U.S. policy.

Reflecting the neoconservative criterion that makes the inviolability of property more important than the right of governments, the bill placed emphasis on the claims for U.S. property that was nationalized in Cuba, even though the U.S. Supreme Court ruled in 1964 that the nationalizations had been legal, recognizing the Cuban government's sovereign rights over the nation's assets. Because of its refusal to negotiate in this regard, the United States is the only country with which Cuba has failed to work out indemnification for its nationalizations.

But the bill went much farther. Due to pressures brought to bear by the Cuban American extreme right, it included as part of the concept of U.S. property that of Cubans who have adopted U.S. citizenship, even when their property was nationalized before they became U.S. citizens. Thus, the bill explicitly proposed to amend the citizenship law of the United States, making it retroactive. If this clause is approved, the problem of indemnification would become impossible to solve, both because of its economic connotations and because of its implications for Cuban national sovereignty.

The bill also stipulated that, in the case of citizens of other countries who invest in Cuba or sign contracts for exploiting property there that might be claimed by the United States, neither they nor their relatives may enter the United States.

Finally, the bill made future relations with Cuba — even with the government that is formed as a result of the supposed modification of Cuba's current political system — conditional on the return of or payment of compensation for that property.

If passed, this bill would force the president of the United States to report to Congress each year on Cuba's trade and financial dealings with the governments and companies of other countries and on the measures the U.S. government has taken to combat those activities — which would mean legalizing economic espionage against Cuba and its trading partners.

Totally ignoring Cuba's sovereign rights, the bill anticipated the overthrow of the present Cuban government and lay down the conditions which the "new political regime" imposed on the country should establish. It also proposed permanent mechanisms for the U.S. government's financing of Cuban governmental institutions.[94]

The European Community, Canada, Mexico, the Caribbean countries, Russia and in effect the entire international community immediately reacted against this proposed legislation, accusing it of violating their own sovereignty, the norms governing world trade, the agreements the United States pledged to support in its free trade agreement with Mexico and Canada and the spirit which should govern global relations in the post-Cold War era.

But, in addition to its implications for the United States' relations with other countries, this bill would set domestic legal precedents in such diverse areas as property, citizenship and the jurisdiction of U.S. laws. Even more important, it would reduce the president's authority in executing the country's foreign policy, thus influencing the general functioning of the U.S. political system.

With regard to Cuba, the bill would affect all citizens without exception, inasmuch as it calls for hauling Cuban society back to the pre-revolutionary era, ignoring the economic, political, social, cultural and demographic changes that have taken place in the last 35 years.

---

[94] "Declaración conjunta Cuba-Estados Unidos" [Cuban-U.S. joint declaration], *Granma*, May 3, 1995, 4.

Whatever happens to the Helms-Burton legislation, the mere fact that it was presented has clearly established the intentions of a sector of U.S. policy-makers, headed by the Cuban American extreme right, on the change they propose for Cuba. A simple reading of these proposals explains better than anything else the depth of polarization on Cuba policy issues in recent years.

New steps toward agreement

Parallel with the discussion of the Helms-Burton bill, Cuban-U.S. negotiations on the migration problem continued. Several meetings were held, in which the two parties recognized that the 1994 agreements had not been fully complied with and took measures to remedy that situation.

The problem of the Cubans living in the Guantánamo Naval Base continued to be a discordant element and an adequate solution has yet to be found. Tensions at the Base have been increasing by the day, and General John Sheehan, Chief of the Atlantic Command, warned of the possibility of rioting and of the increase in spending necessary to maintain order among the refugees in that territory.[95] Both governments were increasingly concerned about the "Guantánamo bomb."

The Cuban American ultraright have made political hay out of the Cubans confined at the Guantánamo Base. The Cuban American National Foundation proposed that they be brought to the United States and be considered as part of the quota of Cuba émigrés allowed in 1994. To help that proposal's being accepted, it suggested that a private welfare program be implemented if the U.S. government would make its policy more flexible and accept around 8,000 people for humanitarian reasons.

For its part, the Cuban government insisted that, according to the agreements, those individuals could not be included in the quota and taken directly to the United States. Such a policy, it was argued, would once again encourage illegal emigration, this

---

[95] Alejandro Rodrigo, ANSA, Washington, May 2, 1995.

time with the incentive of including children and old people in the adventure, since this was how they could qualify under the exceptions to the U.S. regulations. That is precisely what happened: as the spring of 1995 approached, the attempts to leave Cuba illegally for the United States or for the Base increased. The problem was rapidly heading toward a new crisis.

In April 1995, new talks were held in New York and, even though no results were announced immediately that would significantly modify what had already been achieved, on May 2 the two governments announced the signing of an expansion of the agreements, which contemplated the provisional admittance, for humanitarian reasons, of those confined on the Guantánamo Base.

The figure may be as many as 5,000 a year, and they may be included in the quota that was approved in 1994. At the same time, however, the agreement established that from then on the illegal émigrés who were picked up on the high seas would be returned to Cuba and that those who arrived illegally in U.S. territory would be processed for admittance individually, under the laws of asylum in effect in that country. For its part, the Cuban government pledged that it would accept those individuals who were returned and that it wouldn't take any legal action against them — which made it necessary to revise the Cuban laws. Both governments assumed the duty of informing illegal émigrés who were picked up about the procedures they would have to go through in order to emigrate legally.[96]

Janet Reno, U.S. Attorney General, announced her government's decision, emphasizing that those measures represented a new step toward normalizing immigration procedures with regard to Cuba, a humanitarian solution for the situation at Guantánamo and a means for preventing another dangerous, uncontrolled migration from Cuba.[97] Ricardo Alarcón, representing Cuba, noted that this was the first time since the triumph of the Cuban revolution in 1959 that the United States was renouncing its practice of manipulating emigration from

---

[96] "Declaración Conjunta Cuba-Estados Unidos."
[97] Rodrigo, ANSA.

Cuba. He also said that the agreement was beneficial to both parties and that he personally was convinced that the rest of the measures which the Clinton administration imposed in 1994 would be eliminated in the near future, since the crisis situation which had given rise to them had been overcome.[98]

The Cuban American ultraright reacted violently to the accord, some of its members even comparing the decisions with the "betrayal" of the Bay of Pigs.[99] The Cuban American National Foundation expressed its surprise and disgust over not having been consulted, announcing that it would immediately and radically change its relations with the Clinton administration.[100] Congresswoman Ileana Ros declared that, by making that decision and opposing the Helms-Burton bill, Clinton was heading toward improved relations with Cuba. Ros also indicated that the agreements endangered the Cuban Refugee Adjustment Law of 1966. Congressman Lincoln Díaz Balart described the agreement as amazing, immoral and reprehensible.[101] Senator Jesse Helms declared that U.S. ships should be used to blockade and strangle Cuba.[102] Significantly, the top two people in the Office of Cuban Affairs in the State Department resigned in protest against the agreements.

Some noted experts on the relations between Cuba and the United States expressed doubts concerning the Clinton Administration's willingness and ability to implement the agreement and agreed that, if it failed to do so, Cuban illegal immigration would be stimulated more than ever. Jorge Domínguez, of Harvard University, raised doubts about the Administration's political courage. Wayne Smith, of Johns Hopkins University, said that the agreement could not be

---

[98] Marisol Marín, EFE, Havana, May 2, 1995.

[99] The view that Kennedy's refusal to intervene directly in the 1961 invasion amounted to betrayal is widespread in the Cuban counterrevolutionary groups. Some researchers have related this attitude to the possible involvement of Cuban counterrevolutionaries in the assassination of the U.S. President.

[100] Notimex, Miami, May 2, 1995.

[101] Luisa Azpiazu, EFE, Washington, May 2, 1995.

[102] AFP, Washington, May 2, 1995.

assessed without considering its implications for the Adjustment Law of 1966. Andrew Zimbalist, of Smith College, described the measure as strictly economic, without any political meaning at all. Other analysts, both in Cuba and in the United States, viewed the agreement as unfavorable to Cuba, because it annulled its only means for pressuring the United States without completely solving the problem of their relations.

Evidently, the success of the agreements depends on their implementation; this requires a political determination that is in some doubt, because of the indecision and weakness that have characterized this U.S. administration. But the agreements are needed by both countries, and their results reflect the least that could be done to prevent a new migratory crisis.

For the Clinton administration, the Guantánamo situation had become untenable. The administration was being pressured by such dissimilar forces as the Pentagon, human rights groups, the Cuban American community and the Cuban government, all demanding a solution to the problem. Moreover, a new increase in illegal immigrants from Cuba would have been disastrous for the administration just when it was introducing extremely tough bills in Congress against illegal immigration and the immigration question was occupying an increasingly important place in the U.S. political debate.

Illegal emigration cannot be viewed as a tool of Cuban policy. Illegal emigration is unfortunate since, apart from its human implications, it is a destabilizing factor in the island's socioeconomic life and an element that undermines ethical and ideological values. Illegal emigration has already cost the Cuban revolution too much politically. What Cuba needs is stability, and the main merit of the agreements is that they provide just that.

The agreements have an impact on bilateral relations that goes beyond the bounds of the migratory issue. The encouragement of emigration — or hopes of emigration — and exploiting it politically has been a key component in U.S. policy toward Cuba ever since the revolution. The agreements substantially modify that policy, as they transform one of its main ingredients;

in addition, the ideological foundation on which that strategy was based is also undermined. Those who, for one reason or another, are worried about the future of the Adjustment Law of 1966 are justified in their concern, for in addition to governing an immigration procedure this law has been a political tool for challenging the legitimacy of the Cuban system and its relations with its own citizens.

These agreements will also have consequences for Cuba's migratory relations with the rest of the world. Just a few hours before the agreement with the United States was made public, the governments of the United Kingdom, Belize and the Bahamas announced that they had decided to send all illegal Cuban émigrés who reached their territories back to Cuba. It is expected that most other Latin American countries will make similar decisions.

Aware of these implications, the Cuban American ultraright angrily condemned the extension of the agreements. From now on, at least under the law, Cuban immigrants will be treated like all other immigrants in the United States. Since previously they had been given exceptional treatment because of the U.S. government's attitude toward the Cuban revolution, the agreements inevitably influence the thrust of U.S. policy toward Cuba and the role of Cuban émigrés in implementing it.

The degree of this influence and its practical consequences will depend on many factors, first of which is whether or not the Clinton administration can implement its decisions, setting itself against the power that a sector of the U.S. ultraright has attained in designing U.S. policy on Cuba. At least, the agreements have further polarized this debate and limited the role of the Cuban American extreme right in making decisions of the greatest importance for U.S. domestic and foreign policy. The agreements are not irreversible, but at least they weren't drawn up in Miami.

In any case, the agreements were an important achievement for Cuba because they strengthened its position both nationally and internationally. They helped to normalize the pressing migratory problem and encouraged a mentality and a culture that has been the basis of the revolution's ability to stand firm in spite of its difficulties. The agreements also helped Cuba's relations with the émigrés, as their migration was handled with less intransigence, and the Cuban government was able to facilitate the reunification of families.

In this process, the Cuban government demonstrated a willingness to smooth over its differences with the United States, a political maturity in its handling of the crisis, the ability to control the domestic situation without resorting to violence and the fact that it had widespread support for its decisions. The most important consequence of these agreements may well have been for the international image of the Cuban revolution — which, in spite of the collapse of the socialist camp, the U.S. blockade and the domestic economic crisis, is now seen as a relatively stable nation. This stability is very important for readjusting Cuba's international political and economic relations. Therefore, the agreements have already had a positive influence on those trends, both in and outside the United States that favor a change in U.S. policy on Cuba.

To the extent that progress is made in this direction, it will become more feasible to speak of the depoliticization of the Cuban migratory problem, and it will be understood, both by the United States and by Cuba, as simply one more reflection of an international order that by generating inequalities, also generates migration.

Bibliography

Aja Díaz, Antonio. "La emigración ilegal hacia los EE.UU." [Illegal emigration to the United States], *Areíto*, Miami, March 1994.

Alfonso, Pablo. "Clinton pasa a la ofensiva" [Clinton takes the offensive], *El Nuevo Herald*, Miami, August 20, 1994.

Arboleya, Carlos. "Miami's Cubans," *Diario de las Américas*, May 17, 1985.

Arboleya, Jesús. *Las corrientes políticas en la comunidad de origen cubano en Estados Unidos* [Political currents in the Cuban community in the United States], doctoral thesis, Havana, 1994.

— "Las nuevas vertientes de la contrarrevolución cubana: una imagen fabricada para Europa" [New expressions of the Cuban counterrevolution: An image made for Europe], *Revista de Estudios Europeos*, Center of European Studies, Vol. VI, Nos. 25-26.

Arce, Mercedes, *et al. La emigración en Cuba, 1959-1990* [Cuban migration, 1959-90], Department of Immigration and Foreigners' Affairs of Cuba and the Center for the Study of Political Alternatives, Havana, 1991.

Armas, Ramón; López Segrera, Francisco; and Sánchez, Germán. *Los partidos políticos burgueses en Cuba neocolonial 1899-1952* [Bourgeois political parties in neocolonial Cuba, 1899-1952], Social Sciences Publishers, Havana, 1985.

Bach, Robert. "The Cuban exodus: Political and economic motivations," *The Caribbean exodus*, Praeger, USA, 1987.

Booth, Cathy. "Miami," *Time*, autumn 1993.

Brizuela, Roxana, and Fernández-Tabío, Luis. *El potencial económico de las empresas pertenecientes a cubano-americanos en EE.UU.* [Economic potential of the companies belonging to

Cuban Americans in the United States], University of Havana, 1992.

Buckley, William F. "It's a matter of pride," *The Miami Herald*, September 4, 1994.

Castro, Fidel. "Comparecencia ante la televisión cubana el 24 de agosto de 1994" [Appearance on Cuban television on August 24, 1994], *Granma*, Havana, August 28, 1994.

— *Entrevista con periodistas que escriben para la comunidad cubana en el exterior el 6 de setiembre de 1978* [Interview with journalists who write for the Cuban Community abroad, September 6, 1978], Social Sciences Publishers, Havana, 1978.

Castro, Soraya, and Miyar, María Teresa. *U.S. immigration policy towards Cuba: 1959-1987*, José Martí Publishing House, Havana, 1989.

Christopher, Warren. "Declaraciones a la prensa el 13 de agosto de 1994" [Statements to the press, August 13, 1994], EFE, Washington, D.C., August 13, 1994.

— "Declaraciones ante la Comisión de Relaciones Exteriores de la Cámara de Representantes de Estados Unidos" [Statements to the Foreign Affairs Committee of the House of Representatives of the United States], ANSA, Washington, D.C., August 8, 1994.

Contrapunto, Miami, June 1994.

"Conversaciones Cuba-EE.UU.: Comunicado conjunto" [Cuban-U.S. talks: Joint communiqué], *Granma*, Havana, September 10, 1994.

Cortés, Carlos E. *Cuban refugee program*, Arno Press, New York, 1980.

Corzo, Cinthia. "Cambio de la política deja en un limbo la Ley de Ajuste" [Change in policy leaves the Adjustment Act in limbo], *El Nuevo Herald*, Miami, August 20, 1994.

"Cuban Democracy Act of 1992," *Congressional Record*, 1992.

Department of Commerce, Bureau of the Census. *Persons of Hispanic Origin in the U.S., March 1979-October 1980.*

Didion, Joan. *Miami*, Simon and Schuster, New York, 1987.

"Entrevista a José Cabañas" [Interview with José Cabañas], *Granma*, Havana, August 25, 1994.

Epstein, Gail. "Beneficiarios del proyecto Pedro Pan ofrecen homenaje a su benefactora" [Beneficiaries of the Peter Pan project render homage to their benefactor], *El Nuevo Herald*, Miami, June 27, 1993.

Escalante, Fabián. *The secret war: CIA covert operations against Cuba 1959-62*, Ocean Press, Melbourne, 1995.

"Estos datos hablan por sí solos" [These data speak for themselves], *Granma*, Havana, August 25, 1994.

Fonzi, Gaeton. "Who is Jorge Mas Canosa?" *Esquire*, January 1993.

García Agüero, Francisco. "Sector privado teme consecuencias del éxodo" [Private sector fears consequences of the exodus], *El Nuevo Herald*, Miami, September 2, 1994.

Grenier, Guillermo; Gladwin, Hugh; and McLaughen, Douglas. *Views on policy options toward Cuba held by Cuban American residents of Dade County, Fla.: The results of the second 1991 Poll*, Florida International University, Miami, 1991.

Hinckle, Warren, and Turner, William. *The fish is red*, Harper and Row Publishers, London, 1981.

"Información del Gobierno de Cuba a la opinión pública nacional e internacional" [Information from the government of Cuba to national and international public opinion], *Granma*, September 14, 1994.

Jorge, Antonio, and Moncarz, Raúl. *General overview of the Cuban influx since 1959*, The Hague Research Group, 1981.

Judiciary Committee of the House of Representatives of the United States. Immigration and Citizenship Act with Amendments and Notes on Related Laws, Washington, D.C., 1980.

Juridical Affairs Commission of the National Assembly of People's Power of Cuba. *Anteproyecto* de *Ley de Ciudadanía* [Draft of the Citizenship Law], version 4.

Kissinger, Henry. *Years of upheaval*, Little, Brown and Co., Boston-Toronto, 1982.

Lage, Carlos. *Intervención en la conferencia La Nación y la Emigración* [Address in the Nation and Emigration conference], Havana, April 1994.

León Cotayo, Nicanor. *Sitiada la esperanza* [Hope besieged], Social Sciences Publishers, Havana, 1992.

— *El bloqueo a Cuba* [The blockade of Cuba], Social Sciences Publishers, Havana, 1983.

Lernoux, Penny. "The golden gateway of drugs: The Miami connection," *Nation*, February 18, 1984.

Maira, Luis. *América Latina y la crisis de la hegemonía norteamericana* [Latin America and the crisis of U.S. hegemony], DESCO, Lima, 1982.

Masud-Piloto, Félix R. *With open arms*, Rowman and Littlefield, New Jersey, 1988.

Mesa Lago, Carmelo. "Will Cuba's economic reform work?" *Miami Herald*, January 2, 1994.

Miyar, María Teresa. *La comunidad cubana y el tema de las relaciones Cuba-EE.UU.* [The Cuban Community and the topic of Cuba-U.S. relations], CESEU, 1989.

National Security Archives Cuba Documentation Project. *United States-Cuba détente: The 1974-75 initiative and Angolan intervention*, National Security Archives, USA, 1993.

Office of Foreign Assets Control, Department of the Treasury. *New Regulations on Cuba Affecting Mailing of Gift Packages, Travel and Remittances of Funds to Cuba*, Washington, D.C., August 16, 1994.

Osa, José de la. "Califica Alarcón de importancia apreciable acuerdo entre Cuba y EE.UU." [Alarcón describes agreement between Cuba and the U.S. as quite important], *Granma*, Havana, September 10, 1994.

Panetta, León. "Declaraciones a la prensa" [Statements to the Press] AFP, Washington, D.C., August 8, 1994.

Pérez-Stable, Marifeli, and Urriarte, Mirem. *Cubans in the changing economy of Miami*, Interuniversity Program of Latino Research, Boston, 1991.

Pino Santos, Oscar. *El asalto a Cuba por la oligarquía financiera Yanki* [The attack on Cuba by the U.S. financial oligarchy], Casa de las Américas, Havana, 1973.

Portes, Alejandro, and Rumbaut, Rubén. *Immigrant America*, University of California Press, Los Angeles, 1990.

Portes, Alejandro, and Mozo, Rafael. *Patterns of naturalization and voting in the Cuban Community*, Boston, 1984.

Robaina, Roberto. *Discurso de apertura en la conferencia La Nación y la Emigración* [Opening address in the Nation and Emigration conference], Havana, April 1994.

Robbins, Carla Ann. "CIA tells Clinton he could face a crisis in Cuba if serious instability develops," *Wall Street Journal*, November 2, 1993.

Santana, Maydel. "Encuesta: Cubano-americanos rechazan envíos a Guantánamo" [Poll: Cuban Americans oppose sending émigrés to Guantánamo], *El Nuevo Herald*, Miami, August 21, 1993.

Santiago, Ana. "Ni dólares ni vuelos" [Neither dollars nor flights], *El Nuevo Herald*, Miami, August 21, 1994.

Sartre, Jean-Paul. "Huracán sobre el azúcar" [Hurricane over the sugarcane], *Sartre visita a Cuba*, Ediciones R. Havana, 1960.

Taylor, Jay. "Playing into Castro's hands," *Guardian*, London, August 9, 1994.

Thomas, Evan. "Goodbye welfare state," *Time*, November 24, 1994.

Torricelli, Robert. "Carta al Miami Herald" [Letter to *Miami Herald*], *El Nuevo Herald*, January 5, 1994.

Wyden, Peter. *Bay of Pigs: The untold story*, Simon and Schuster, New York, 1979.

Also published by Ocean Press

ISLAND UNDER SIEGE
The U.S. blockade of Cuba
by Pedro Prada
Cuban journalist Pedro Prada presents a compelling case against this
"last wall" of the Cold War, showing how the 35-year blockade has
affected life in the tiny island nation.

**THE CUBAN REVOLUTION AND THE UNITED
STATES**
A chronological history
Second, expanded edition
by Jane Franklin
An invaluable resource for scholars, teachers, journalists, legislators,
and anyone interested in international relations, this volume offers
an unprecedented vision of U.S.-Cuba relations. This updated,
second edition includes detailed coverage of U.S.-Cuba events up to
the end of 1995.

GUANTANAMO: THE BAY OF DISCORD
The story of the U.S. military base in Cuba
by Roger Ricardo
This book provides a detailed history of the U.S. base from the
beginning of the century until the present day.

ZR RIFLE
The plot to kill Kennedy and Castro
Second, expanded edition
by Claudia Furiati
Thirty years after the death of President Kennedy, Cuba has opened
its secret files on the assassination, showing how and why the CIA,
along with anti-Castro exiles and the Mafia, planned the conspiracy.
*"Adds new pieces to the puzzle and gives us a clearer picture of what
really happened."* — Oliver Stone

Also published by Ocean Press

IN THE EYE OF THE STORM
Castro, Khrushchev, Kennedy and the Missile Crisis
by Carlos Lechuga
For the first time, Cuba's view of the most serious crisis of the Cold War is told by one the leading participants. Rushed to New York during the crisis to take up the post of Cuba's ambassador at the United Nations, Carlos Lechuga provides a coherent history of what really occurred when the world was on the edge of a nuclear catastrophe. Lechuga also reveals exclusive details of his participation in a secret dialogue between Washington and Havana immediately prior to the assassination of President Kennedy, discussions that could have led to a thaw in U.S.-Cuba relations.

THE SECRET WAR
CIA covert operations against Cuba, 1959-62
by Fabián Escalante
The secret war that the CIA lost. For the first time, the former head of Cuban State Security speaks out about the confrontation with U.S. intelligence and presents stunning new evidence of the conspiracy between the Mafia, the Cuban counterrevolution and the CIA. General Fabián Escalante details the CIA's operations in 1959-62, the largest-scale covert operation ever launched against another nation.

CIA TARGETS FIDEL
The secret assassination report
Only recently declassified and published for the first time, this secret report was prepared for the CIA on its own plots to assassinate Cuba's Fidel Castro. Under pressure in 1967 when the press were probing the alliance with the Mafia in these murderous schemes, the CIA produced this remarkably frank, single-copy report stamped "secret — eyes only." Included is an exclusive commentary by Division General Fabián Escalante, the former head of Cuba's counterintelligence body.

Also published by Ocean Press

FACE TO FACE WITH FIDEL CASTRO
A conversation with Tomás Borge
The issues confronting a changing world are frankly discussed in this lively dialogue between two of Latin America's most controversial political figures.

AFROCUBA
An anthology of Cuba writing on race, politics and culture
Edited by Pedro Pérez Sarduy and Jean Stubbs
What is it like to be Black in Cuba? Does racism exist in a revolutionary society which claims to have abolished it? How does the legacy of slavery and segregation live on in today's Cuba? *AfroCuba* looks at the Black experience in Cuba through the eyes of the island's writers, scholars and artists. The collection mixes poetry, fiction, political analysis and anthropology, producing a multi-faceted insight into Cuba's rich ethnic and cultural reality.

CUBA: TALKING ABOUT REVOLUTION
Second, expanded edition
Conversations with Juan Antonio Blanco by Medea Benjamin
A frank discussion on the current situation in Cuba, this book presents an all-too-rare opportunity to hear the voice of one of the island's leading intellectuals. Juan Antonio Blanco is the director of the Félix Varela Center, a non-governmental body in Cuba dedicated to the study of ethics and politics. This updated, expanded edition looks at new issues that have arisen in Cuba in recent years.

THE GREENING OF THE REVOLUTION
Cuba's experiment with organic farming
Edited by Peter Rosset and Medea Benjamin
The first detailed account of Cuba's turn to a system of organic agriculture, prepared on an international scientific delegation and fact-finding mission on low-input, sustainable agriculture which visited the island in late 1992.

Also published by Ocean Press

CUBA: REVOLUTION AT THE CROSSROADS
by Fidel Castro
What future lies ahead for Cuba's revolution as it approaches the
new millenium? Has the revolution failed? Must it now turn its
back on the past four decades? In a series of speeches during 1994-95,
Cuban leader Fidel Castro discusses the main issues confronting the
small Caribbean island as it tries to adjust to a changing world.

CHE — A MEMOIR BY FIDEL CASTRO
Preface by Jesús Montané
Edited by David Deutschmann
For the first time Fidel Castro writes with candor and affection of
his relationship with Ernesto Che Guevara, documenting the
Argentinian-born doctor's extraordinary bond with Cuba from the
revolution's early days to Che's final guerrilla expeditions to Africa
and Bolivia. Castro vividly portrays Che — the man, the revolut-
ionary and the thinker — and describes in detail his last days with
Che in Cuba.

THE FERTILE PRISON
by Mario Mencía
This is the story of Fidel Castro and his young comrades, including
two women, when they were imprisoned after the July 26, 1953
attack on the Moncada military garrison, and how the Batista
dictatorship was eventually forced to release them. Included in this
volume are many documents such as Castro's letters from prison,
published for the first time, as well as an extensive glossary and
chronology.